NOAH ZAN

INSIGHTS INTO

INFLUENCE

THE STRATEGIES, TACTICS, & SECRETS OF WORLD-CLASS LEADERS & SOCIAL SCIENTISTS

INSIGHTS INTO INFLUENCE

The Strategies, Tactics, and Secrets of World-Class Leaders and Social Scientists

ISBN 978-1-951317-05-8

Published in the United States by Weeva, Inc.
First Printing, 2020

Editing by Weeva, Inc. and Quantified Communications
Cover design by Weeva, Inc.
Interior design by Weeva, Inc.

Weeva
701 Brazos Street
Austin, TX 78735
www.weeva.com
Hello@Weeva.com

bookstore.weeva.com

DEDICATION

First, to my family—Anna, Sawyer, Elle, and Miles—who have encouraged and loved me through it all.

Second, to all the contributors in this book, whose advice, stories, and lessons are the essence of the book.

Third, to all the future leaders: may this book help you accelerate your path to improving the world.

Foreword

Life is about persuasion. Navigating our pathways through childhood, school, profession, and marriage, to name just a few, is largely a matter of effectively persuading parents, teachers, admission officers, bosses, and spouses. So, given the importance of these chapters of our lives, you could say that our overall happiness and success in life is dependent on our ability to persuade. And yet, persuasion doesn't get much attention or credit.

I have spent most of my professional life helping elect candidates to various offices in government, and five times I've been the chief media consultant to candidates who've won presidential primary and general election contests. Elections are the ultimate act of persuasion. I've spent countless hours trying to figure out what, specifically, people running for office need to do to persuade voters to support them. And there is much I've learned over the years about what techniques are effective. I'm a right-brained guy, and all my observations about what works are entirely subjective and anecdotal.

Whether you supported Donald Trump or Hillary Clinton or someone else for president in 2016, consider this notion, with which I think people on all sides of the aisle would agree: On paper, Hillary Clinton was easily one of the most experienced, most prepared, and most qualified people ever to run for president. She was a former First Lady, United States Senator, and Secretary of State, and she was running against someone who'd never held a single elective office in his life. But she was a lousy persuader. And she ran against a guy who had a very successful television show and who understands the power of persuasion.

As important as persuasion is to life, to love, to politics, to business, it's incredible that, until now, no one has really applied science and analytics to understanding how, why, and when it works. Enter Noah Zandan. I had the opportunity to work with Zandan early in his career, and I knew immediately he was someone special who was going to make some great contributions to our society. He's developed a successful business bringing analytics to persuasion, and now he has written a book exploring this subject that, despite being so important, has been left unexplored and unexamined for way too long.

There is a lot of evidence that to get ahead and be successful in life these days, you should spend some time thinking about persuasion. And Noah Zandan is here to help.

MARK MCKINNON
Creator and Cohost of Showtime's documentary series, *The Circus*

Introduction

Ten years ago, I asked myself a question: What's the difference between me and the global leaders I respect? The people who move the world with their words and their actions: Martin Luther King, Jr., Winston Churchill, Steve Jobs, Oprah Winfrey, Mahatma Gandhi. We all agree on who they are, but ask anyone what makes their favorite leaders so influential, and that's where the answer becomes cloudy. Is it what they speak about, how they say it, simply what they stand for, or something else?

It turns out this is a hard answer to obtain, much less put into practice.

I've spent the last decade obsessively searching for insights. Early on, I encountered two big sources of frustration. First, self-evaluation is an unreliable guide. Do I inspire people? Do I motivate them? How do others perceive me? I wanted a more objective way of defining my starting point and my progress.

Secondly, despite the huge number of amazing books and research studies on influence, most felt outdated or too theoretical. I wanted applied, prescriptive, and current knowledge.

So I decided to produce my own.

A New Roadmap to Influence

In the ten years since I started my search for the keys to influence, an exciting change has happened. We began to understand how to quantify intangible human qualities like influence.

Thanks to innovations in machine learning and technology, humanity at large has made huge strides in the fields of behavioral science, neuroscience, and audience decision-making analysis. These advances have allowed us to study human behavior, interaction, and audience response like never before.

With these new capabilities, we're finally in a position where we can define concrete, specific insights about what makes iconic leaders so powerful.

This book consolidates those insights into a new, actionable roadmap to influence. I spoke with twenty global experts to gather diverse perspectives on influence in action. From politics to money to sex to entertainment to brain science to C-suite leadership, we gathered the freshest thinking and most actionable behavioral recommendations.

Quantifying Influence

We expanded on these experts' insights by gathering and analyzing the world's most comprehensive data set on leadership communication. To be honest, while we wanted to see what we could discover with data, we didn't know what we would find. As I set out to create this book, I was nervous about comparing my firm's behavioral science data with the insights gained from experts and leaders. Would the findings be consistent?

I am delighted to report that the insights, research, and perspectives of the contributors to this book mesh extremely well with the data. I am even more excited that by combining the data with practical application, we found a few surprises to share. Those behavioral tactics are the missing quotient to solving the influence equation.

Use This Book to Reach Your Potential

This is a book I wish I had read when I was in college, when I was twenty-three and just starting my career on Wall Street, and when I was twenty-nine and a CEO for the first time. This is a book written for all the leaders and future leaders who, on their journey to elevating human connection, seek to become extraordinary communicators and reach their full leadership potential.

Between the data, the experts, and the field-tested experience, we have produced a book that unveils what it really takes to be influential. Here's the key takeaway: Influence can be learned.

I hope this book accelerates your journey to achieving your aspirations, whatever they may be.

NOAH ZANDAN

Table of Contents

"You can't set out with the goal of being influential; it's a bad goal. Influence is a means to an end."

Adam Grant is recognized as Wharton's top-rated professor and has been among Fortune's 40 under 40. He is the author of three books on *The New York Times* Best Seller list: *Originals*, on how individuals champion new ideas and leaders fight groupthink; *Give and Take*, on why helping others drives our success; and *Option B*, co-authored with Sheryl Sandberg, on facing adversity and building resilience.

His TED talks on the surprising habits of original thinkers and the success of givers and takers have been named the best of 2016 and 2017 and received more than ten million views in two years. He hosts "WorkLife with Adam Grant," a TED original podcast, and is a contributing op-ed writer on work and psychology for *The New York Times*.

Influence Is an Outcome, Not a Goal

Adam Grant

Let's start at the top. As a recognized expert in organizational psychology, what factors do you think have helped you achieve influence in your field and in your practice?

I'm an academic, so being a tenured professor has been key. I've also built credibility through organizations I've worked with, books I've published, and pieces for *The New York Times*. That backdrop tends to capture a wide variety of people's attention. As far as why people are drawn to my ideas, well, that varies.

I'd say my best ideas, the ones people really latch on to, share three main qualities. I think of it as a Venn diagram. The first circle of the diagram is "interestingness"—ideas that intrigue by either challenging conventional wisdom or reinforcing a prior but not fully understood belief. The second circle would be "evidence." That's what differentiates me from many others in my arena: I have rigorous data backing up my key arguments. And then the third circle would be a sense of utility or "practical application." My most influential ideas are at the center of the diagram, where all three qualities overlap.

When I think about the reputation that you've built, your expertise, you seem to be on every channel. Most university professors aren't able to, or at least don't, leverage their expertise in that way. In a way, you have taken university

research and made it into a lifestyle brand. Was that a conscious decision?

Yeah, I mean, that was part of why I became a social scientist in the first place. I can't imagine studying human behavior without wanting whatever knowledge I produce to be useful to humans.

When I was in college and taking psychology courses, the ones I found the most interesting were the ones that didn't just turn my world upside down but also gave me tools to use in the real world. At one point I was working in advertising sales for the *Let's Go* travel guides. At first, I was really terrible at it. But then I took a psychology class where I learned key concepts about persuasion. I applied Cialdini's[1] principles at work and suddenly found that I was much better at my job. The learning was immediately useful.

That sort of practical application is what fascinated me about some of psychology's great field experiments, the ones that improved the quality of people's lives or solved social problems. For instance, Elliot Aronson's jigsaw classroom experiment. That led to a reduction of prejudice in recently desegregated elementary schools in Texas. Each student had a piece of what was required to complete the project. When they had to work toward a common goal and depend on one another, it became harder for them to view a fellow student as someone they might look down on or as a member of a lesser group. They started to see each other as human beings.

I kept coming across interesting experiments like that, that took insights from psychology and made them practical and meaningful for people. I thought they were awesome. Donald Stokes's book *Pasteur's Quadrant* had a huge impact on how I thought about this. He says most people think research lies on a continuum. At one end is basic research, or people doing pure science, and at the other end are research practitioners. The common conception is that you can't do both. You can only be on one end of the spectrum or the other.

But Louis Pasteur's work just blows that theory apart. His first big discovery led to germ theory, a field that we can safely say has saved millions if not billions of lives, and he did it while practicing applied science for an industrialist. The point is you *can* do both.

Of course that brings to mind the area of study you're so well known for: improving our work-life balance. How does that relate to what you're talking about?

Oh, directly. What I did was bring the *Pasteur's Quadrant* takeaway to organizational psychology. Most people take it for granted that you can't be really successful at work and enjoy a fulfilling life. I wanted to find a way to collapse that

1 Robert Cialdini. *Persuasion*, Harper Business, 1984.

spectrum—just like with research and applied science, they're not mutually exclusive goals. Most of us spend a majority of our waking hours at work, yet far too few of us find that time meaningful and motivating. I wanted to generate and disseminate ideas and evidence that could make work better for people by combining the two dimensions. At a minimum, I wanted to make work suck less.If I can get leaders to care about my ideas, if I can get entry-level employees to build momentum around ideas, I feel like I'm making work more meaningful and motivating. I'm using my influence to achieve a broader goal.

So we come back to this idea of having influence in the first place...what advice would you give someone who was trying to be more influential? Are there any techniques you suggest?

The thing is, you can't set out with the goal of being influential; it's a bad goal. Influence is a means to an end. A lot of people overlook that. They want to be influential because it connotes importance, status, notoriety—but most people don't want to be influenced. We like to be in charge of our own destiny. So ask yourself the question, "Influence for what? Why is it important to me to be influential?"

If it's extremely important to you to merely be influential, that often backfires. You end up pursuing these very instrumental ways to try to reach people as opposed to saying, "How do I invest in doing really good work?" You prevent yourself from

"Most of us spend a majority of our waking hours at work, yet far too few of us find that time meaningful and motivating. I wanted to generate and disseminate ideas and evidence that could make work better for people by combining the two dimensions. At a minimum, I wanted to make work suck less."

offering something that matters. If you don't care about what you're doing in itself, if your only goal is "influence," how can you expect to get others to care about it?

And keep in mind that influence is largely local rather than global. There are very few recipes that work in every organization or in every line of work. When you enter a new orbit, ask people who already have the influence that you aspire to, "What are the things that have enabled you to have an impact and be valued? What are the ways that people have tried to have influence around here that have backfired?" Learn the local norms, and identify some role models to emulate and maybe some to avoid.

Once you know *why* you want to be influential, then you can take action.

As you've worked with leaders in an applied way to make organizations better and to make work better, is there anything you've discovered around influence that's really surprised you?

Well, the thing is, to successfully influence people to change, you need to bring them fresh insights. That's always going to come with surprises. I've always felt like the value of social science is that we test people's intuition. You can either challenge their existing beliefs or build on them in order to test their intuition. Often we can identify where their beliefs are wrong or incomplete.

When you do that, though, you often get resistance. I remember going into an investment bank to figure out how they could get better at attracting and retaining junior analysts and associates. I had a lot of former students who were miserable in those jobs, and I knew they had a problem. I wanted to see if there was anything we could do to improve their experience of work.

I spent a couple of months on research. I performed a combination of experiments, surveys, interviews, and observations, and then of course I also reviewed evidence from studies of other workplaces and other industries. I came back with twenty-six recommendations. I summarized my report for the co-heads of investment banking, and one of them said, "Well, I understand you want to make the work more meaningful. You want to give these people learning opportunities and let them see the clients instead of just hiding out in an office with spreadsheets. But why don't we just pay them more?"

I hated that exchange. If there's one way to threaten my core professional identity, it's to completely ignore the data. Plus, it's something they should already have known: they were paying people much more than other fields would have done, yet that wasn't enough to keep employees around. Both the outside data and the internal data were converging on the message that this problem was not solvable with just money.

I realized that, in order to gain credibility, I had to do the exact opposite of everything I'd been trained to do. Rather than just provide data, I needed to confirm his intuitions *first*. That's how I would make myself credible. So I came back to the next conversation saying, "There is a lot of evidence that one of the most important influences on whether people want to take a job, and then whether they'll stay in it, is whether they feel like they're paid fairly for the work they do. So if you want to look at how to adjust pay to accomplish that, I'm happy to support you. I know you've tried that before, so I'm curious: where has that approach fallen short?"

All of a sudden, the tone completely changed. Now I was hearing, "You know what? You're right. Pay is really important, and we have worked really hard to calibrate it. Here are all the barriers we face to making that the attractor and retainer we need it to be. So we'd love to hear what else might make a difference." It opened the door to sharing the insights that were, to at least this particular banker, less intuitive.

Can this sort of approach be institutionalized? If confirming someone's intuition works to establish trust so you can maybe influence them, it seems like it could be a good method to get people on board with new initiatives internally.

Absolutely. For instance, in the work that I've done with Google, they very often start their projects by collating really obvious research for their own engineers. For example: "If you want to be a better manager, greet your employees on their first day, and make sure they meet their boss face-to-face, one-on-one."

Rocket science, right? But it's something that every engineer can relate to, and it's easy to overlook. It's something they may have personally felt was missing when they were onboarded in the past. So, they try it out, and they find that people really appreciate it. They also learn that people don't like *not* being greeted on their first day. Now the people analytics team has earned a reputation for delivering credible and immediately actionable insight.

Once you have built some trust, then you start to earn what Edwin Hollander would have called idiosyncrasy credit, where you have the license to deviate a little bit because you've proven your value. It gives you a little more latitude to say, "Your ideas are useful and workable, even if they're obvious. What else do you have?" You get permission to go out on a limb and show them something different. If you want to challenge people's beliefs and influence them to change, one of the best things to do is start by confirming their beliefs.

You used to perform as a magician. Has that had an impact on your work today?

Magic definitely taught me some valuable lessons about relating to audiences. I've carried that into almost all the work that I do, especially speaking and teaching.

I'd say my biggest takeaway is that it's incredibly important to be aligned with your audience on what the goals are. A magic trick doesn't work if your audience doesn't want to be fooled. There's an implicit contract between a magician and an audience. The magician's goal is to create a sense of mystery; the audience's goal is to be mystified.

I've found that idea of creating a common contract immensely important in dealing with any audience.

Sometimes it's not possible to know your audience's goals, of course, like when you're giving a speech or creating a piece of writing. I try to make my own goals explicit in each book so that at least my part of the contract is clear. "Here's my objective. What I want to do is convince you of the following. What I want to do is show you why I changed my mind about this topic, and why you might want to as well. I want to introduce you to a new way of thinking about this topic."

Magic also taught me that it's rarely the trick itself that hooks the audience. What gets them is the patter, the story you tell, the way you prepare the audience to expect one thing and then see another. It's another approach—nearly the opposite of saying something obvious to get skeptical audiences on board with you. If you want to intrigue people with what you have to say, it's sometimes helpful to set up the expectation that one thing is true and then show them why something else is true instead.

I see this over and over again when people try to translate psychology. Look at the Google finding that psychological safety is a key ingredient for successful teams. When people think it's safe to take a risk in a team, they innovate more—another bit of rocket science, right? This information is in danger of being easily dismissed because it feels so obvious, but it's critical information that deserves serious consideration. It can be presented in a way that feels exciting and brings new insight.

Could you provide an example of how obvious information could be presented in a way that makes it feel fresh?

I can actually give you a very good example with that innovation theme. Let's go back to the idea that teams vary in psychological safety. In some of them, it's really safe to take a risk: you won't get in trouble if you speak up with a crazy idea, raise a problem, or admit an error. And then there are other teams where, if you make a mistake, somebody will bite your head off. If you suggest an idea that's contrarian or countercultural, you'll get silenced pretty quickly.

One study of hospitals seemed to show that the more psychological safety teams have, the more errors they make. Why would that be? Well, you could imagine that when it's safe to take a risk and you don't worry about getting punished for mistakes, you might not double check your work, and maybe your teammates don't double check your work either. It's dangerous when accountability falls apart.

But this researcher at Harvard, Amy Edmondson —she does amazing work on teams and leadership—took a closer look at that study and found something interesting. The data on the errors were reported by the teams themselves. So were they making more errors or simply admitting to them?

“It's rarely the trick itself that hooks the audience. What gets them is the patter, the story you tell, the way you prepare the audience to expect one thing and then see another.”

“Why rely on imagination when you have access to so much personal experience at being the audience? People try to influence you every day. There's a wealth of insight to be gained by comparing and contrasting the times when it's worked to the times it hasn't.”

To get more objective error data, she used a covert observer to report when mistakes were really made.

The new data revealed that psychologically safe teams do, in fact, make fewer mistakes. They just own up to them more. When team members disclose their errors rather than hide them, others can learn from them. They don't repeat the same mistakes over and over again. It turns out that psychological safety, which might have at first seemed dangerous or to lead to sloppy behavior, is in fact essential for learning.

Isn't this a much more compelling way to be introduced to that information? That reveal strategy is something I first learned in magic.

For those of us who haven't been professional magicians, can you offer any advice to spark up our influence tactics?

Approaching any sort of communication with an entertainment mindset can help an audience be more receptive to your ideas. Humor is a great tool. Evolutionary psychologists have written about this, saying that one of the supposed evolutionary functions of laughter is to signal safety. If I can get people laughing, they're less defensive when I share something that might challenge their beliefs. When I use something funny in class, like stories or clips from *South Park*, I notice that students are more engaged. It puts them in a more curious mindset as opposed to a defensive or cynical one, and that's what you want: to leave them curious.

But honestly, the best way to learn to get better at influence is to treat yourself as an audience member. Ask yourself, "The times that I've been most influenced by somebody else, what did they do? What did they say? How did they get through to me?" We all have a hard time imagining ourselves in the audience's shoes. So why rely on imagination when you have access to so much personal experience at being the audience? People try to influence you every day. There's a wealth of insight to be gained by comparing and contrasting the times when it's worked to the times it hasn't.

When I'm influenced the most, it's not first and foremost because I think the information is credible. It's because I think the source is credible. I listen to people I trust, and then I start to evaluate. If a person hasn't already intrigued me and impressed me with their credibility in some way, then the argument or the idea often falls on deaf ears.

We spend too much time trying to formulate the perfect pitch. Instead, focus on building a relationship with the audience. Establish trust and credibility. That's when they'll be open to your ideas. That's the path to influence.

EDITOR'S NOTES

Grant suggests that confirming your audience's intuitions before delivering fresh insights is key to influencing them. This dovetails with Ethan Burris's discussion of surfacing people's assumptions and then challenging them to rethink their perspectives.

“Being persuasive and influential is not an end goal. What is an end goal is being persuasive and influential in a direction that you want to see the world head.”

Franklin Leonard is the founder and CEO of the Black List, which supports great screenwriting and the writers who do it via film production, its annual survey of best unproduced screenplays, an online marketplace, live staged script readings, screenwriter labs, and film culture publications. Black List movies have won over fifty Academy Awards from nearly three hundred nominations.

Leonard has worked for Universal Pictures and the production companies of Will Smith, Sydney Pollack and Anthony Minghella, and Leonardo DiCaprio. He was featured as one of *The Hollywood Reporter's* "35 Under 35," *Black Enterprise* magazine's "40 Emerging Leaders for Our Future," *The Root's* "100 Most Influential African-Americans", and *Fast Company's* "100 Most Creative People in Business." He received the 2015 African-American Film Critics Association (AAFCA) Special Achievement Award for career excellence and is an associate professor at the American Film Institute.

Intellect, Integrity, Inquiry

Franklin Leonard

When was the first time in your life that you realized you were influential?

I grew up in West Central Georgia, and we went to an Episcopal church every Sunday. We were the only black family that attended—otherwise it was an all-white congregation. I remember being taught things about the church's point of view that I thought were illogical or deeply problematic. I remember asking questions of my Sunday school teacher that I knew would lay bare the inconsistencies I was seeing, and I remember my fellow Sunday school classmates beginning to have more questions as a result.

That's the first time I can remember thinking, "Oh, I can inject something into this system that changes the way the system functions." Now, it wasn't grand or world-changing, but I think that my fellow fifth graders' worlds were shaken by the notion that maybe what we learn in church isn't literally the Gospel.

That's how I think about influence: it's one person's ability to change another's point of view.

From that moment onward, what factors do you think helped you the most to achieve the influence you enjoy today?

Integrity is critical. People know that what they're getting with me is an honest, thoughtful, rational approach that has been deeply researched. I think I've established a personal brand built around those things, and people are more willing to be influenced by me because of that.

“That’s how I think about influence: it’s one person’s ability to change another’s point of view.”

Communication style has been really important, too. I've synthesized this hyper-analytical, quasi-amusing, somewhat confrontational style of communication that I think people enjoy. People are willing to take their medicine when it comes with a little bit of sugar. Over time my early opinions have been proven right, which helps. If you have a record of saying, "This is going to happen," and then it happens, people are going to be a lot more interested in paying attention to you when you next say, "You should look at things this way."

People aren't influenced by me because I'm attractive or my Instagram is particularly interesting. Although, to be totally honest, my appearance may be a factor. People can be fascinated by the hyper-analytical, deeply academic approach that I take when I look like I do, with dreadlocks that extend to my mid-back and a full beard. There is an unfortunate assumption that people who look the way I do don't talk or think the way I do. I have a friend who says, "To some people you're this weird Rasta magician who talks like an economist." Even if I would like to disassociate those things, the perceived contrast can act as a draw.

How much of your identity as an influencer do you actively think about and try to develop, and how much is the result of natural progress?

It comes to me naturally. To the extent that I do think about it, it tends to be in the context of having to make a public statement. In that case I want to make sure the point of view I express is pretty much bulletproof for debate purposes.

I don't want to criticize someone else's point of view unless I've carefully considered all the ways in which they might come back at me and thought through my potential responses. Some of that is just self-protection—I'm not trying to get caught out in these Twitter streets making a fool of myself—but I also think that being right matters and being deliberate matters. I want people to be able to trust that I'm not throwing out a statement offhand. I want them to expect my points of view to have been deeply considered.

Who's had the biggest impact in your life along your path to influence?

I look to people in culture who engage politically, those who are highly visible and have not shied away from speaking truth to power. People like director Ava DuVernay and activist Brittany Packnett have guided how I shape my public voice.

I also have tried to learn from people in the political realm who carry themselves with a high degree of integrity and honor—and oftentimes take a lot of shit for it. Whether it's Brittany Packnett or Alexandria Ocasio-Cortez, I really admire those folks, some of whom are younger than I am, in terms of how they are able to wield influence with the aim to make the pie bigger and create more access for other people.

More to my personal brand, especially on social media, I also really admire comics who bring a high degree of intelligence, along with a vernacular that is very much of the streets and of the people, to marvel at the ridiculousness of the world. The most recent example of this is Desus and Mero. They just started a talk show on Showtime, and they've had a podcast for years. They have rapier wits and are deeply engaged in the world around them, and they're literally just two dudes from the Bronx who sit and talk about shit. They are ridiculously funny, and their brains work so fast. It would be very easy to dismiss them as two dudes from the hood, but then they'll drop a line about Michael Cohen. These guys are living and synthesizing both high and low culture, and that is very much a part of who I am.

Can you say more about generating influence through humor?

It's very difficult to convince anybody of your point of view if you're coming down on them hard. You don't want to be this sanctimonious bore. One of the most compelling things about making your argument is doing so on the merits of the case, but on some level you also want to imply, "Yo, it's more fun over here with this point of view," too.

I'll end up in these situations on Twitter where I'm talking about a political issue or about a politically adjacent issue in the film industry, like diversity and inclusion, and someone will start trying to have an argument or troll me. I immediately come back with comedy while still making the argument. It's disarming to people who want to be mad at you, and then they can actually seriously consider your point of view.

One of my prouder moments was on a flight back from San Francisco. Some conservative college kids were tracking down photos of me and making memes of me for being a crazy liberal. Instead of being angry about it, I started playing them against each other. Like, "Oh, does Texas A&M not have a graphic design department? Because your dude at University of Texas did a much better job with his." Or like, "Oh, I grew up in Georgia, where we have a pretty fine sense of aesthetics. I don't know what it's like in Oklahoma. Maybe you should go back and take a senior year art class again."

By the end they were laughing with me and making fun of each other, and literally every single one of them ended up following me. From time to time they still comment in funny ways about things we have in common. I'd much rather have that scenario than have them label me as some sanctimonious, easily triggered lib.

Can you talk about social media as a tool of influence in your career?

Social media has allowed me to be influential and to be influenced by people who are far outside of my immediate professional and social locus. It was very easy for me to develop a profile for myself in Hollywood by making and taking phone calls, making and taking meetings, and reading material and giving valuable feedback on it, but outside of that very narrow part of the industry, no one was ever going to know who I was. I was the person behind the person behind the camera. Social media, Twitter in particular, has given me

an opportunity to express my point of view to the world, to have people judge me on my own words, and that's where I've figured out what my public persona is: highly political, highly engaged in culture, and hopefully a little funny.

How do race and gender play into influence?

It cuts both ways. I have benefited by being black on Twitter, where this community I'm part of has given me a great following. I think that's true for gender too. We tend to be drawn in and attracted to people with whom we believe we have shared experiences. People talk about me as one of the important voices in Black Twitter, and while I think there are many, many more important voices than mine in that community, it's an honor to be part of it.

Now, the flip side of that is that you're also going to get a lot more trolls. Those college students wouldn't have shown up in my mentions if I were a liberal white guy. I know that for the black women and for queer people of color I'm close with on social media, it's even worse. In a weird way, though, even the negative attention that you attract is, on some level, beneficial for your influence in the long run; you don't get trolls unless you're making some progress in advancing a point of view.

Outside of social media, it's definitely harder to be a person of color or a woman. How many panels have we seen that don't feature either? How often are people unconsciously discounting what you've accomplished by 40 percent, 80 percent, because they just can't conceive that a person who looks like you can be as valuable as a white man who hasn't done half of what you've done? In my sleep I could be more valuable in five minutes than some film industry panelists can be in an hour, but they're the ones getting invited to speak. I say that with no ego but just as simple fact.

What accounts for the disparity? The short answer is racism. And there are women who are not invited because of racism and sexism. I think we need to call these things what they are. If you can't find women or people of color to talk about the issues that you ostensibly think are important, odds are it's your failure and not the failure of these broad communities that represent roughly 75 percent of the population.

As society progresses toward a better understanding of the importance of diversity and inclusion, do you think that model might flip toward people being more influenced by outside opinions and less by confirmation from their own group?

I do have hope for that. People are starting to wake up to the notion that while, yes, inclusivity is a moral and ethical imperative, it is also a financial one. Companies and leaders who embrace inclusion tend to perform better. Certainly film and television that embrace diversity and inclusion do better at the box office. So, I'm optimistic for somewhat cynical reasons. I'm optimistic about that change because I have great faith in people's desire to make money.

What advice would you give a young, smart, driven person who wants to be more persuasive and influential in the real world—and what advice should they ignore?

What to ignore is easy: follower count. Don't worry about quantity as much as quality. Ignore anybody who tells you that influence and being an influencer is an end in its own right. It's not. In fact, the pursuit of influence for the sake of influence is, I think, one of the most dangerous realities in contemporary life.

Being persuasive and influential is not an end goal. What is an end goal is being persuasive and influential in a direction that you want to see the world head. First decide what kind of world you want to see. Then figure out who you are and what you're comfortable with in terms of a public persona.

Once you figure those two things out, it becomes a lot easier. Then it's just about how you elevate that point of view to as many people as possible. You'll be more compelling coming from an authentic place of integrity than a construct like, "Well, I need to be influential to make more money." It's a lot easier to reach people when you have a personal, deeply held belief and a real sense of self-awareness about who you are in the world. Figure out who you are—and what you actually believe.

If you had to put up a gigantic billboard about influence, what would you want it to say?

Funnily enough, Desus and Mero have a version of this at the end of every show. They ask, "If you had a neon sign in a bodega, what would the neon sign say?" Mine would say, "Conventional wisdom is usually all convention and no wisdom."

EDITOR'S NOTES

Like Leonard, Grant and Pohlson cultivate humor as a tool for influence. Crockett echoes Franklin's emphasis on integrity in her discussion of understanding values.

> **"Conventional wisdom is usually all convention and no wisdom."**
>
> **—Franklin Leonard**

"An influential person is not somebody who is perfect. It's somebody who is able to give you enough value that the balance between effort and reward is worthwhile."

Dr. Carmen Simon is a cognitive neuroscientist, author, and founder of Memzy, a company that uses brain science to help corporations create memorable messages. Carmen's most recent book, *Impossible to Ignore: Create Memorable Content to Influence Decisions*, has been selected as one of the top international books on persuasion. Carmen holds two doctorates and teaches at Stanford University. She holds frequent workshops for corporate audiences on the importance of using brain science to craft communication that is not only memorable but sparks action. After all, what's the use of memory if people don't act on it?

First, Be Memorable

Carmen Simon

Tell me about the fascinating work you do.

The neuroscience question I've been focused on building my career around is, "What does it take for the brain to remember something, especially given a business context?"

On the surface that might be an easy question, but in reality it is a damned difficult question to answer. We're gaining more understanding about how the brain works, but we're still far away from decoding this mysterious organ. We throw terms like "neurotransmitters" and "dopamine" around as if we've known about them for ages, but we haven't. Neurotransmitters were only identified about a hundred years ago. Much of how the brain works remains a mystery.

Memory is particularly elusive and complex. It takes one memory system to remember that you had a fun vacation in Paris, yet another to remember that you felt something toward the person you were with during that vacation. It takes another memory system to remember that Paris is the capital of France and yet another to ride the bicycle that you perhaps rode to go get your croissant. I like the fact that we haven't decoded everything about how the brain works yet. It makes my job much more fun.

How do you relate memory to persuasion and influence?

You cannot persuade anyone unless you are enabling them to remember you. I know that's a strong statement, but we can make it because we recognize that every action that the brain enables you to do is based on what you remember. Whether you're remembering consciously or subconsciously is a different story, but every single movement that you make toward an idea, product, service, or person is driven by your memory.

When you ask how to be more persuasive, you're implicitly asking how to be more memorable. But here's something a lot of people don't realize: while we tend to equate "memory" with what neuroscientists call "retrospective memory," or remembering your past, the type of memory that is actually more important here is "prospective memory," or remembering to act on future intentions. This is very important in business or as you're considering how to build your own influence. You have to ask the question, "Will people remember me in the future?"

So, what are the different factors that drive memory in a positive way?

Honestly, we don't have a complete answer to that yet. I can tell you, though, that three of the core variables that determine how well your brain will remember a given experience are intention, reward, and repetition.

Intention is powerful, but it requires a plan and action to succeed. Let's say that you and I want to sell our services to a client and we have a great meeting. The client is thinking, "Oh, this is a good idea. I intend to do something about it." The intention is there, but will they actually hire us? There's often a big gap between intentions and action. We need to influence some particular variables in order to stay on the client's mind once we're no longer in the room.

One of these variables is the quality of the reward. If you're trying to get somebody to meet with you again, say in order to see your demo, that requires them to make an effort. The brain asks if such an effort is worthwhile, and a reward is what makes it seem worthwhile. What my company has observed of people we work with is that, quite often, the reason they're forgettable is because the reward is either not clear enough or not strong enough.

Disney has nailed the strong reward idea. When somebody promises you access to the happiest place on the planet, the reward is very clear and very enticing. It makes movement toward it worthwhile. And obviously, Disney has big budgets to remind us of that reward. But it doesn't take a huge budget to have strong clarity around a reward; the constant reminder is what takes a whole lot of budget and time. You can get around it without a million dollars.

Here's an example from something I'm working on right now with a B2B company, which is a category that often struggles with being memorable. I asked, "What's the reward that you're promising to your audience's brain? Why should they move in your favor later on?" They said they promise they will put their clients' IT infrastructure pieces together.

The phrase "We help you put the pieces together" sounds good in theory, but you're making me work too hard to understand what you're really doing for me. Are you making my business more efficient by putting these things together? Are you saving me money? Are you making it easier for my customers to access my solution? It invites too much speculation; there's no way to know which one is right or most important.

If the clarity of the reward is not strong, the intention is not going to be there, and the action falls back.

What makes a strong "memory" reward? How do I create a great one?

It helps to know what motivates your audience. Of course, different brains crave different rewards—just think of how much food cravings can vary by person—but there are such things as universal rewards. Whether you're in Austin and craving barbecue or I'm across the country and craving chocolate, I guarantee you that we would both respond to the promise of controlling our own environment, looking good in front of other people, freedom from worry, safety. We're driven by aesthetics, prominence, curiosity, and often by novelty.

I was once asked to create a presentation for the two scientists who won a Nobel Prize for stem cell procedures. When I walked into their office, they showed me their presentation. It was made up of some of the ugliest slides I had ever seen. But I was so humbled. When they asked me if I could make it better, I said no. No PowerPoint effects or aesthetic technique would have made a contribution to what they were talking about. There was so much that was new and thrilling in what they were proposing that no one was going to notice, say, colors not matching on the slides. That's how the power of novelty can supersede many other things.

Home shopping channels exploit the concept of novelty very successfully. They might market a rock from Armenia with a sexy fancy name that in Armenian just means "rock," but because they're packaging it to make it seem completely new, you're just drawn to it. We are biologically driven to newness because a brain that does not explore is not a brain that survives.

"Three of the core variables that determine how well your brain will remember a given experience are intention, reward, and repetition."

Could you say more about that third factor you mentioned, repetition?

This is such an important one. Just because we remember something one time does not guarantee that we'll remember it forever. And your degree of influence, to me, would be the longevity of memories you're putting in your audience's brain.

We are all often guilty of a particular kind of arrogance: we think that meeting with somebody once will create a long-lasting memory. I would invite all of us to be humble about this. Creating a long-lasting memory from one experience is what science would call learning from a single trial, which is much more difficult than learning from multiple exposures. In life there are very few things that lend themselves to single-trial learning. An accident, a strong and shocking thing to the body, may stay with you, but a chart in a PowerPoint slide? Not unless it's the PowerPoint of a Nobel Prize-winning stem cell researcher, and very few are.

There's no magic number of times something must be repeated before your brain remembers it. Simple things might only need to be repeated a few times, while more complex ideas could take six, seven, eight, nine times or more. For instance, if your spouse asked you to buy barbecue on your way home, asking you more than once or twice would go beyond influencing your memory and right into annoyance. But contrast that against trying to learn a technical or business concept, like blockchain. The first time you hear the word, you have no idea what it is. And then somebody else mentions it, and somebody else mentions it again, and somebody else mentions it again. Each time it takes less effort for the brain to wrap itself around the idea.

Competition is also very helpful to prolonging memories in your audience's brains. In a competition, other people are presenting similar things as you, so you're not relying on single-trial learning anymore. Repetition is the mother of memory, and therefore the grandmother of influence. So when you have competition, don't dismiss it. Welcome it.

So competition is a good thing for memory?

Yes. Because competition gives you the luxury of repetition, we can discover yet another memory variable: distinctiveness. While competition does the work for you in terms of moving beyond single-trial learning, you're aspiring to have people remember you distinctively compared to others.

So in business or society or politics, from your perspective who is influential?

One of the classes that I teach is the science of storytelling for business. As I was doing a lot of research on what it takes for a story to be memorable, I read about this guy who said that he remembered his second grade teacher who taught him that stories are not natural. Stories are your ability to put order into what's otherwise chaotic and meaning into what's otherwise meaningless. Stories don't happen in real life. We're *told* stories in real life. The guy was probably in his mid-fifties,

and I thought how powerful that he would remember something fairly detailed and insightful from his second grade teacher. I think many teachers are unsung heroes of memory.

I've been listening to Malcolm Gladwell's MasterClass course over and over again. I'm intrigued by him because I think he's one of the worst speakers I've ever heard. He doesn't complete his ideas—but on the other hand, he has good ideas. So if you're willing to overlook some technicalities, you can learn from him. An influential person is not somebody who is perfect. It's somebody who is able to give you enough value that the balance between effort and reward is worthwhile. Gladwell is a good example of someone hitting that balance.

Do you notice him using any particular techniques that get people to remember him better, making him more effective?

Actually, yes. He twists the familiar in a pleasant way, which is another variable we know contributes to creating memories. Gladwell says as a guideline for becoming a better writer, add candy to your writing—namely, parenthetical or tangential statements. So, let's say you're speaking about an outstanding business person who did very well for himself and then you add, "Oh, and by the way he's the guy who is responsible for the way that coupons are created in the United States."

That parenthesis didn't do anything to the writing, but because of it you may remember the writing. It makes the entire process a lot more pleasant and interesting. It's not like Gladwell is telling us something new by giving this advice. But the way he twisted something that we already know feels fresh and helps us remember that story.

Are there any other memory factors you would like more people to know about? Anything we're missing?

Well, there is one big thing I could add: In order to influence someone's memory, make sure that you influence your own first. Sometimes when I work with executives, I realize that they report on somebody else's memory, not their own. For example, one exec was telling me about disruption in his industry. I asked him what he meant, how that reflects his own experiences. He shared with me a trip that he took with his son to a train museum. The photos were so sweet; his son was maybe ten years old and smiling big with braces on, wearing shorts and looking at these trains. And it was while looking at these trains that his father was able to reflect on how much his company had disrupted the transportation industry when it first appeared, and how much they've been disrupted in turn lately.

By interjecting his own memory onto that story, the exec was able to help me remember that story clearly. I can't tell you how many times I've heard executives talk about "disruption in their industry," but this one stuck with me. Laying your own memory (like the trip to the train museum) on top of some content that has been given to you by somebody else (like data about disruption in your industry) makes listening to you more worthwhile and memorable for your audience.

Carmen, I'm going to give you a billboard that millions of people will see every day. What would you like that billboard to say about influence?

You know, I would probably take a saying from a poster my team and I made that's currently hanging in my office. It says at the top, "Memory moves the world." And you can see in the poster this little VW van with a giraffe sticking its neck out from behind the wheel. The text at the bottom says, "Find your memory lane." We associate the phrase "a trip down memory lane" with remembering the past, but it's a two-way street. There's no reason that memory lane can't lead to the future.

To master the art of getting people to remember you in the future, utilize the variables that affect how well the brain remembers anything: Make sure that the reward you're promising your audience is strong enough and clear enough. Repetition is critical. Find some distinctiveness to what you're offering so people remember you instead of your competition. Try offering novelty, or a way to twist the familiar. These are what will get you remembered, and that's influence.

EDITOR'S NOTES

Kadlubek, whose work is the definition of novelty, expands on Simon's "power of novelty," adding insights about the importance of structure to give spontaneity its power.

"Memory moves the world."

—Carmen Simon

“Laughter is the shortest distance between two people.”

Matt Pohlson is the cofounder and CEO of Omaze, the online fundraising platform that offers people the chance to win dream-come-true experiences and opportunities in support of causes around the world. Under Matt's leadership, Omaze has raised over $100 million to directly support charities by making it fun and easy for people to give back. These fundraising and awareness campaigns bring together influencers, nonprofits, and donors from over 180 countries to create real, lasting impact.

The Value You Bring

Matt Pohlson

You've built a very influential platform that's doing amazing things. What factors have helped you most to achieve the success and influence that you have?

At Omaze, we view our capacity to influence simply as a function of how much value we can create for others. Talent and charities agree to partner with us if we can drive significant funds and awareness for their work. Donors agree to contribute if we provide them experiences that excite them and connect them to the causes they support.

In order to understand what your partners value, you need to be a good listener. You need to ask the right questions and practice empathy.

I was an actor for a couple of years. I wasn't very good at it, but I learned valuable skills around empathy. Your whole goal as an actor is to see the world through the eyes of your character. When I transitioned to writing, I did my best to create a consistent "why" for my characters' actions. You can never know exactly where someone is coming from, but if you take the time to try to understand and then ask clarifying questions, you can start to build a bridge.

At Omaze, we've tried to codify the importance of empathy into principles. When we were a four-person startup, we had to influence the busiest people in the world to come work with us without any track record. We constantly evolved our pitch and our approach into three simple steps: (1) demonstrate that you understand your audience's priorities, (2) establish credibility, and (3) own the next action step.

When you're first starting, you establish credibility through proxy. In other words, we used the fact that President Obama has used the same fundraising model successfully as evidence that what we were proposing would work. Owning the next action step is really about making it as easy as possible for your partner to take the next step.

How do you communicate that you understand your audience's priorities? What does that look like?

You ask questions, listen to the answers, and constantly summarize what you hear to confirm you really understand.

Once you're confident you've reached a shared understanding, then you can start to use storytelling to create a common vision.

For example, we consistently ask our customers what they are looking for from an experience. We know they want quality time with the talent, they want to do something that will be fun to share with their friends, and they want to have a clear vision of where the money is going.

So when we did a partnership with Arnold Schwarzenegger, rather than making it a meet and greet, we offered the chance to ride in a tank with him and crush things. We made a fun video to show our customers what that would look like and introduce them to the kids who would benefit. The video got over fifty million views, and we raised over $1.1 million for After School All-Stars.

Similarly, when we were working with Kobe Bryant to create an experience around his last game, we knew that he wanted to raise as much money as possible for his foundation while also accommodating his incredibly busy schedule.

We shared the story of how we'd faced similar constraints with Tom Brady, another athlete he admires and who is also incredibly busy. We showed him how we'd done a video with Tom quickly after practice one day and had limited the setup to make it as time efficient as possible. But because Tom was so funny in the video, it had generated over one billion impressions, raised over $1.3 million for his foundation, and ended up airing everywhere from *SportsCenter* to *The Today Show*.

Kobe agreed to do something similar.

Interesting. So, humor can play a role in getting people on board with your vision. Can you expand on that?

Absolutely. Humor is an incredibly powerful tool for creating connection. One of our core values at Omaze is that laughter is the shortest distance between two people. And that drives our methodology behind our content. If you can get people laughing first, they are much more likely to pay attention to your message.

A lot of time in the charitable world, filmmakers default to telling stories about the despair of an issue and nothing else. When we did the Clinton Foundation's Decade of Difference television and concert event, they encouraged us to take another approach. They were addressing incredibly serious issues around HIV, climate change, job growth in the developing world, malaria, and many other initiatives. They wanted those stories told in a way that honored the gravity of the issues, but they also wanted to reach a younger audience. So President Clinton agreed to be part of a video with a bunch of comedic talent, which ended up driving more awareness for their work than any other video they'd done before.

But humor doesn't just have to mean large-scale comedy. Being able to simply laugh at yourself is also important. When people think about influence, they can get caught up in their egos. They hold onto a certain idea of status as the way to influence people. Self-deprecation can be an incredibly powerful tool to break through that, to bring people together and establish trust.

Speaking of self-deprecation: Let's say I want to come off as credible and confident and respectful. How can I also be self-deprecating?

One could argue that being self-deprecating and vulnerable makes you more credible. One of our core values at Omaze is that we take our work seriously, but not ourselves. When you share stories of times you've made mistakes or when you were embarrassed, it makes others feel more free to be vulnerable in return. We all know that we are imperfect human beings. But sometimes we get so caught up in the personas that we've created for ourselves that we forget to keep it real. It's especially important to demonstrate that vulnerability when you're in a leadership position so that the people working for you feel comfortable to make mistakes.

"You can't communicate value unless you're clear."

What if humor feels off-limits to you? For instance, because you think you're not funny?

I believe everyone has the capacity to use humor. Some people think you're born funny or not funny. You're born musical or not musical. These are not binary conditions. They are ranges. Certainly some people are more naturally talented than others, but sense of humor, like musical ability, is a skill that can be developed over time.

One way to learn is just by consuming it. Listen to people who are funny having conversations. Listening to Marc Maron interviewing all his comedic buddies helped make me a better comedy writer. You just get a sense of how these people talk in real life.

But going back to where we started with humor, it's really about creating trust by being vulnerable and self-deprecating. It's less about telling jokes and more about having the ability to laugh at yourself. And anybody can do that.

You have obviously discovered great ways to foster connection and generate influence. At your company, do you ever run into instances where that's not enough and you have to use tactics of influence?

It really depends how we are defining tactics. There are certainly ways of presenting information to people that do a better job of communicating the value you can create for them. For example, empowering third parties to speak to your value is a powerful tool. We often ask partners to talk to previous partners rather than take our word for it.

Or, when facing a question a partner is asking, we explain how another partner may have addressed it. At one point we had some pushback from a legendary band on how we wanted to approach a campaign—they wanted to send traffic to their site instead of ours. We explained that another band who they respected had a similar question but ultimately decided to send the traffic to Omaze because our site was optimized for collecting these types of donations, and the fundraiser could have raised $1 million to $2 million less if not done properly. Walking through the thought process of a third party was much more effective than just offering our reasons.

Contrast can also help create clarity, and you can't communicate value unless you're clear. The human mind needs to constantly triangulate and compare. So when we were first explaining our model, instead of saying, "We raise money and awareness for charity by offering the chance to win once-in-a-lifetime experiences," we'd add that others typically handle this like an auction where one high-net-worth individual pays $25 to $50 thousand to hang out with Bryan and Aaron from *Breaking Bad*. But in our model, we can raise $1.7 million with the same experience. If we had only told how much we raised, people would have a harder time understanding the comparative value.

I'd like your advice. Let's say I'm a smart, driven person who wants to be more persuasive and influential in the real world. What do you tell me to do, and what do you tell me not to do?

The famed communication coach Nancy Duarte once said that the biggest mistake public speakers make when they present is that they make it about themselves rather than the audience. They assume they are the heroes standing up to endow the audience with wisdom. The most influential speakers take the opposite approach. They make the audience the hero. They recognize they are Yoda, and the audience is Luke Skywalker.

That rule applies to leading people, to selling products, parenting, and to anything else that you do where you are asking someone to work with you.

All right. One more thing. I'm going to give you a billboard that millions of people are going to drive by every day. What would you have it say about influence?

Create value for others.

EDITOR'S NOTES

Pohlson identifies humor as a foundational tool for influence, and this theme recurs throughout this book. He also cites the importance of listening deeply; Bartlett, Crockett and others expand on this insight, while Minson adds the important dimension of openness to new perspectives.

"Create value for others."

—Matt Pohlson

"It can reduce the intensity of a conversation to keep in mind that humans agree on a lot more than we disagree on."

Julia Minson is an associate professor of public policy at the Harvard Kennedy School of Government. She is a social psychologist with research interests in conflict, negotiations, and judgment and decision making. Her primary line of research addresses the "psychology of disagreement"—how do people engage with opinions, judgments, and decisions that are different from their own?

Julia is the organizer of the Colloquium on Research Results in Advancing Leadership (CORRAL) speaker series and is the faculty director of the Harvard Decision Science Laboratory.

Prior to coming to the Kennedy School, Julia served as a lecturer at the Wharton School, University of Pennsylvania, where she taught Negotiations at both the MBA and the undergraduate levels. She received her PhD in social psychology from Stanford University and her BA in psychology from Harvard University.

Openness is the Key to Influence

Julia Minson

How would you describe what you study to a nonexpert, a layman?

I study when and why people are open to views that are really different from their own, which could be in the domain of hot-button political topics like gun control, abortion, or immigration, but could also be in the domain of lifestyle choices. Is it a good idea to have children or not? Should you be married or single? Are dogs or cats better? In a professional context, it's about how you work with colleagues who come from different professional backgrounds and have different professional priorities: software engineers versus marketers, advertising versus finance. The key questions are how you engage with people who have different priorities than you and how you maximally benefit from what they have to say.

My colleagues and I have developed a scale we call "receptiveness to opposing views" that measures how likely a particular person is to engage with opposing views. We assess this with a five-minute, eighteen-question agree/disagree questionnaire. It seems to predict pretty well how likely people are to expose themselves to information they disagree with, think about it carefully, and then evaluate it using the same criteria they would use for information that supports their own beliefs.

So we know how to measure this tendency to engage with opposing views. The question is, can this tendency be increased? One thing we've found is that when people show receptiveness by listening intently in conversation, it makes their counterparts more receptive. Which is cool, because it's much easier to control yourself and demonstrate open-mindedness, and perhaps get some in return, rather than to force your conversation partner to do so first.

Let's say you're a Massachusetts liberal and I'm a Texas Republican and we're talking about politics. How do I actually practice the receptiveness you're talking about in that conversation?

Pay attention to the sort of questions you're asking. In these conversations, question-asking is huge, yet people often ask the wrong ones. Questions that are a statement or a counterargument with a question mark at the end—like "What kind of idiot are you to believe X, Y, and Z?"—are not helpful.

What you want to ask, instead, are what I call "elaboration questions" that signal a curiosity and desire to understand. "What led you to have those beliefs?" or "How do you interpret this particular piece of data?" will get you a lot further if you truly want to understand someone else's views. Understanding where someone is coming from is key to influencing them to go where you want them to go.

There's a very famous social psychologist, Ellen Langer, with whom I studied as an undergrad. She once said, "You know, Julia, people always do something because it makes sense to them. Everything people do makes sense to them at the time." At first that sounds like a tautological truism, but really it's very deep.

It speaks to another common mistake: assuming that someone doesn't agree with you because you know something that they don't, and if you just educate them properly they'll come to see it your way. That comes across as incredibly condescending. It's important to recognize that people have different reasons for their beliefs. As a function of your circumstances, upbringing, gender, family, and so on, certain things matter to you that don't matter to another, and certain things matter to another that don't matter to you.

These conversations aren't as unpleasant as we expect them to be, either. (This is something we now have evidence for, thanks to new research from my colleagues Charlie Dorison and Todd Rogers.) A Massachusetts liberal talking to a Texas Republican might expect an awful experience fraught with negative emotions, yet when we actually put people into those kinds of conversations in our studies, it's not nearly as bad as they expected.

The reason we misjudge it is often because we overestimate how much we disagree. That Massachusetts liberal sitting down with the Texas Republican will turn out to agree on a surprising number of things. Sharp points of disagreement really stand out in our minds, but similar values frequently underlie them. It can reduce the intensity of a conversation to keep in mind that humans agree on a lot more than we disagree on.

As a recognized expert in your field, what factors helped you the most to achieve the success and influence you enjoy today?

The main thing that has helped me achieve success and become influential in my field is how open to being influenced I've been. From high school through my post-doc, I had really brilliant people giving me the information and support I needed to grow. What I can take credit for is truly listening to them.

There are many generous people out there, but to really reap the benefits they offer, you need to show your willingness to learn. You have to invite that influence and show appreciation for their mentorship. This is especially important when it comes to hearing constructive or downright negative feedback.

Talk to me about how you actually stay open to opposing views. How do you show somebody you appreciate their negative feedback?

Nobody likes to be in the situation of offering negative feedback. It requires going out on a limb interpersonally—it's an awkward place to be. But if you can signal that you're someone who will appreciate that feedback, implement it, and grow from it, then that's different. For instance, a graduate student might ask for feedback and hear, "This isn't particularly novel or good. You should go back and start from scratch." That's unpleasant, but the right thing to do is to send that person a thank you note. Tell them the reasons their feedback was thought-provoking and let them know you've now read the following papers or made the following changes as a result of what they've said. And then ask to meet again and get *more* feedback.

Responding with gratitude and demonstrating that you've really taken in the feedback is very different from offering an insincere thanks and skulking out of the office. What you want is for them to think of you as the kind of person who's open to suggestions. That way if they have something major to tell you in the future, they might be more willing to do it.

Being open to feedback from others requires you to be honest with yourself. That sort of openness and authenticity is so critical to achieving real influence. You have to be able to understand and clearly communicate your goals and preferences. Part of that is giving feedback as well as receiving it: let people know when they've done a great job or are working hard, and provide some course-correction if someone isn't on track.

If you're authentic about what you're trying to accomplish and why you think it's important, and if you celebrate and reward the people who are advancing that goal while correcting the people who are not, your job becomes much easier.

What criteria would you use to identify an influential person?

I think about influence as leadership: it's the quality that gets other people to hold opinions and engage in actions that are in line with your goals. You could be the mom who got your toddler to put his shoes on or the leader of a social movement who got thousands of people to march on Washington. The common ingredient is that you had a goal and you got other people to do what you needed them to do in order to accomplish it. It all comes down to clarity and consistency.

This is the question I'm most excited to ask you. What are the factors that drive influence when you're talking to an engaged, agreeable audience versus an audience with opposing views?

In those two situations, your goals would be different. Because if the audience agrees with you, then you're presumably influencing them toward action. You don't need them to agree with you more. You need them to do something about the agreement. Whereas if the audience disagrees with you, then the first thing you need to do is either get agreement or at least get them to stay out of the way.

So, those are two different problems. There is a lot of research on how you get people in that first bucket, who basically agree with you but who need to take action, to follow through on the behavioral intentions they already have. So do I want people to stop buying plastic water bottles? Or do I want people to vote, or to vaccinate their kids? Let's say you're working with a bunch of educated Massachusetts liberals who all agree that water bottles are bad and voting is good. But the fact is most of us still buy water bottles and half of us don't vote.

The issue here is translating intentions into actions. There's a lot of work on nudges to get people to do what they already want to do. I would turn to the research on this for more depth; there's great work out there from Todd Rogers, my colleague here at the Kennedy School and who I mentioned before, and from Katy Milkman at the Wharton School at UPenn.

Now let's turn to the bucket of people who disagree with you. Are they passively disagreeing or are they in active opposition? Because if people are passively disagreeing with you but not doing anything harmful or obstructive to your goal, trying to persuade them could be a waste of your time. Just say, "Okay, you disagree with me, fine. Just stay out of it then we're cool." We have such a need to convince other people that we're right that I think we spend a lot of time persuading people who can't or don't need to be persuaded.

What about those in active opposition? Do you have any tips for influencing them other than what we've gone over already?

Sometimes the trick to achieving what you want is just knowing when to quit selling. That requires having really good clarity about your goals as an influencer.

The main course I teach is on negotiations. The theme we spend the most time talking about is really understanding your goals. A lot of people go into a negotiation with very vague goals or allow them to be changed as a function of the conversation. For example, imagine that you want a new role at work. You bring all your arguments to your boss and then she says, "That's a great idea. You can have that assignment because honestly, I don't think you're doing very well in your current role."

If you're like most people, you wouldn't celebrate the fact that you just got exactly what you wanted. Instead, you might respond, "Oh no, let me have another six months in this role. Let me prove to you that I'm actually really good at this." But that wasn't your goal. Your goal was to get the new assignment. Now you got it, so shut up and stop selling.

All right, I'm going to give you a giant billboard to get a message out about influence. What does it say?

When you disagree with somebody, especially if it's on a matter of fact, you should always remember there's a 50 percent chance that you're wrong.

EDITOR'S NOTES

Franklin Leonard, Helen Fisher, and Derek Kilmer also discuss how to relate to people with different points of view. Like Minson, Gil Eyal, Dianna Kokoszka, and others drill home the absolute non-negotiability of being your authentic self.

"When you disagree with somebody, especially if it's on a matter of fact, you should always remember there's a 50 percent chance that you're wrong."

—Julia Minson

“The foundation of influence is trust. You build trust by being honest, and you build trust by being honest over time.”

Will Hurd, a San Antonio native and Texas A&M computer science graduate, was excited to spend his entire career serving his country by stopping terrorists, preventing Russian spies from stealing our secrets, and putting nuclear weapons proliferators out of business as an undercover officer in the CIA—until he realized that his expertise in cybersecurity and intelligence was sorely needed in Congress.

Since being elected in 2014, Will has blazed his own trail to deliver bipartisan results by working with anyone, regardless of politics and party, to help make sure our kids are ready for the future, that our country is safe, and that the United States will always be the leader of the free world.

Texas Monthly and *Politico Magazine* called him “the Future of the GOP.” His efforts to put good policy over good politics have clearly struck a chord in a country that is often consumed with what divides us instead of what unites us.

Do the Right Thing

Will Hurd

As a member of Congress, how do you define influence?

When I think of influence, I think of effectiveness. Can you have an effect on somebody else's behavior and on their actions? To me the term "influence" is similar to "leadership." It's a quality that other people bestow on you, rather than something that you claim for yourself.

How do you think about influencing others? Moving them to take action toward your goals?

I look at this strictly from my position as an elected official. Every two years, I'm trying to get a certain number of people to do something on a certain day. So, that's measurable. Outside of an actual election, you have to ensure that your constituents see you as someone who is representing them. Am I delivering on the particular issues that they care about? But also, knowing that many issues may be clouded by misunderstanding, am I able to clarify the issues for people and, potentially, change their minds?

How connected do you think my behavior is on election day with how effective you are around the issues I care about?

I think there's a direct correlation. My desire on election day is that when someone goes in that booth, they're thinking, "Who is going to best represent me?" If they're thinking about anything else, then I'm going to have a difficult time that day.

And someone only gets to that point when, over time, they've felt like I've represented them well. That means a whole lot of things. Do they see me showing up in the community? Have I been right on enough of the issues? Have we agreed on enough of the issues?

I always say the election is determined the year before. The 2020 election is decided in 2019. Ultimately, you have to build a relationship with your voters. You can't do that in the ninety days leading up to a vote. It takes consistent effort, work, and engagement.

How conscious are you of how you build your own influence? How much do you strategically write down and have a plan for, and how much do you feel you gain naturally through your experience?

I think the key to influence is that you have to have a message. You have to craft it well, and you have to have the right mode to deliver it. For me, that mode is different leading up to an election and during one. Choosing where to deliver the message, whether it's social media or op-eds or so on, that's deliberate. And *how* you deliver the message, once you understand what that message is, matters too. For instance, I've recently switched up my speaking style. I'm usually very extemporaneous, but I've tried to start being more disciplined with the flow of my speeches.

As you strategize on your political influence, how do you think about the division of time between crafting the message and delivering the message? I'll give you one hundred points to distribute between the two—how do you prioritize?

I would say crafting the message is probably 70 percent.

Take a recent example. The Clint Detention Facility is in my district. This has been in the news. I have my own opinion on what we need to do when it comes to dealing with the crisis at the border. However, I wanted to do my homework. I needed to meet with all the border sector chiefs. I wanted to meet with some lawyers working on the issue. I had to go in and inspect the facilities myself. It was important for me, too, to try to understand the Department of Homeland Security's perspective on this.

So in this process, I needed to get some ground truths, figure out what I feel is the right thing to do, see how that meshes with the facts we gathered on the ground, and then come up with real long-term solutions, which are what no one seems to want to talk about on this issue.

The question is, how do I move people from their current understanding of the issue to where I think they need to go? That takes time, that takes energy, that takes effort. That's where I would say 70 percent of the task is knowing what you're going to talk about. Delivering the message is often easier because you already know what points you're going to make.

Wait, let me get this straight: you believe the public doesn't want to hear about solutions, just the problems? Do you think that's because the American public just doesn't have the patience for that conversation, or that they're overwhelmed with media and distractions?

I do believe the American people are open to discussing real solutions. I think there are two interesting trends right now: attention spans are getting shorter because we're just bombarded by so many other things, yet long-format podcasts are growing in popularity. You have to keep that in mind when thinking about the mode for delivering your message. You have to be able to boil it down into a six-second sound bite, but you also need to explain in depth.

Let's go back to the more fundamental influence questions. Who has been influential in your life and career?

People I follow and look up to because I think they're effective might surprise you. They're people like Jerry Seinfeld. He focuses so completely on his craft, obsessing over one word versus another. He tells a great story about how it took him two years to write one joke. The joke is funny, but him telling how it took him two years to write the joke is funnier. When you look at being able to get someone to laugh for as long as he has, words matter. Process matters.

I like Arthur Brooks from the American Enterprise Institute. He talks about issues of the day in a unique way. Anytime he says something, it kind of expands my mind. I also admired John McCain: he was in the public spotlight so long, and yet was able to maintain an identity as an independent thinker, a maverick. That's really important to me.

Those are people who I try to learn from, though that's not the only form of influence. You could say the most influential people in my life have been my mom and dad. My dad always told me to be honest, to treat people with respect, and that the one person you can't fool is the person you're looking at when you're brushing your teeth in the morning. My mom taught me that you shouldn't care what other people think about you; the only thing that matters is what you think about yourself.

You mentioned Jerry Seinfeld's obsession with every word. Among all the influential leaders you admire, what patterns do you see?

The foundation of influence is trust. You build trust by being honest, and you build trust by being honest over time. Expertise can also earn you trust. The people I mentioned not only have an expertise, but they have been honest over their careers, and they've shown a level of consistency. I think they're able to deliver a message that gets at and addresses people's motivations.

One thing I learned from my days in the CIA is that you don't recruit somebody to commit espionage unless you can understand what their potential motivations are to do that. For me, a lot of my conversations start with trying to determine the other person's motivations to think the way they do or care about a particular issue.

Understanding someone's motivations won't necessarily leave them open to being influenced by you, though. That's where trust comes in, which you build through expertise and consistency. When I first came to Congress, I had a disproportionately large influence on security matters because I was seen as an expert. I was the only freshman legislator who had ever started a cyber security company, had a degree in computer science, and had ten years as an undercover officer in the CIA. I was able to talk about cyber security issues, national security, and foreign policy issues and be taken seriously. Now, because I have more border in my district than any other member of Congress, I'm the leading voice on this issue.

I like how you're breaking it down between motivations and trust, as well as consistency. We've heard a lot about how authenticity generally promotes consistency.

Yeah, I think authenticity is, are you the same person over time? My old chief of staff would always say the audio and the visual need to match. Does your behavior reflect the things that you're saying? Are you demonstrating consistency over time? When you do, that's how you get people to make a decision when they go into the voting booth.

You're known for your bipartisanship. Talk to me about influence within the political realm as you balance what you believe in, what's expected from you by the party, and what your voters want. How do you decide what to do? What makes you effective?

It's actually really easy. Just do the right thing. At the end of the day, I was elected to represent roughly eight hundred thousand people. Collect the information about the issue, make a decision on what needs to be done, and then go out and explain to people what you're doing. My job is to do the right thing. I always start with that.

Then it comes down to explaining myself based on all those factors that you just outlined. I might explain the same thing a little differently to different people; the message stays the same but gets fine-tuned for the audience.

I'll make sure my first point of a message speaks to the bulk of my audience. Let's say there are five things that I think are the most important points to get across—A, B, C, D, and E. Sometimes I may lead with A, sometimes I may lead with E. It depends on the audience, but I'm still going to get through all five of my points.

You want to lead with the thing that most people are probably going to agree with you on, get them to nod their heads and say yeah, okay, I agree with that. Then you get through your other points that may be new ideas to them, or something that they don't necessarily agree with.

I'd like your advice. I'm a young person, I want to be effective, I want to create influence, I want to lead people. What should I do?

Go out and have a career first. Develop expertise so that you have a reason for people to listen to you. Then once you do that, make sure the audio and visual match. Make sure you're consistent over time. Seek to understand before being understood. Spend time trying to understand an issue, and when you're talking to people, try to learn what your audience is actually seeking. When you know that, you can figure out what could potentially be a gift for them, how you could benefit them.

“The question is, how do I move people from their current understanding of the issue to where I think they need to go?”

When it comes to your message, be like a comedian: test that message out. Deliver your message to a friend and see how they respond. Then do that with a small group, just a few people. Then if that works, do it in a larger group. Don't bring it to a big group until you have some idea of how it's going to land.

How much do you actually test? If you've got something new you want to share, where does it really start?

I do this every day. I went and got a coffee today from my favorite shop in Helotes, Texas. I was talking with the owner and a regular, and they asked a question. I thought to myself, "I'm going to see how they'll respond to this." I made the point, and they were like, "Oh, interesting, I didn't know that." So now I'll probably use that point in a larger group to see how multiple people respond to it. Maybe that line will end up in an op-ed I write on a particular topic. Then that will be one of the key points in a speech that I make.

Honestly, on any particular issue, especially if it's a new issue or new idea, I'm constantly trying it out and getting people's feedback on what they think about it.

I believe we see your computer science background shining in there a little bit.

Absolutely. I test, test again, and see how people respond. There have been times where I've said something on the stump and people laughed, and I didn't know why. If I try it again and still get the same reaction, okay. I'm going to keep using that line. People laugh at it.

Trying to get a point across takes practice, forethought, and planning. Again, you have to make sure you have the right message, and then you can focus on the delivery.

I'm going to give you a billboard in whatever jurisdiction you want. That means that people are going to drive by it every day. What do you want it to say?

"Be honest." It's that simple.

Even if someone doesn't agree with you, at least they're going to walk away and be like, "You know, I appreciate that person's honesty." In a time when getting real facts is even harder than it used to be, even though we have so much information at our fingertips, people really appreciate simple honesty. It's almost a new sensation.

When you listen and you're honest with people and you show up, it does change people's opinions. I always tell this story about visiting Eagle Pass, Texas. The first time I showed up was at an afternoon party with about seven hundred people there. I was literally the only Republican. Three of the members of the band were local officials, and they actually stopped playing when I walked in, because everybody was like, "Why are you here?"

My answer was because I like to drink beer and eat cabrito too. Then when I showed up the second time, people actually shook my hand. The third time, people told me their problems. The fourth or fifth time I showed up, people walked by and whispered, "I'm a Republican." Then I kept showing up, and I was able to tell them, "Hey, that problem that you told me about a while ago, here's how I was able to fix it." That's why I went from 16 percent of the vote in Eagle Pass to 21 percent to 27 percent. That doesn't seem like a lot, but when you look at how many more people are voting to get that number to increase each time, in such a tough district, that's a tectonic change. And a lot of that is simply showing up and listening to people and being honest.

EDITOR'S NOTES

Hurd sees trust and relationship building as foundational to influence, and many others echo this perspective. Without trust, there can be no influence.

"Be honest."

—Will Hurd

“You can’t expect people to be there for the landing if they aren’t there for the takeoff.”

Derek Kilmer serves as United States Representative for Washington State. Born and raised on the Olympic Peninsula, the son of two school teachers, Derek saw firsthand how economic struggles affect working families and their communities. He studied economic development, earning degrees from Princeton and Oxford.

Through work for McKinsey & Company and the Economic Development Board (EDB) for Tacoma-Pierce County, Derek gained an appreciation for how government impacts the ability of private sector companies to succeed and grow. He has received the Heroes of Main Street award from the National Retail Foundation and the Outstanding New Member Award from the Voices for National Service.

Derek was elected to serve in the Washington State House in 2004 and to the Washington State Senate in 2006. He lives in Gig Harbor with his wife, Jennifer, and their daughters, Sophie and Tess.

The Art of Collaboration and Flexibility

Derek Kilmer

As a current member of the US House of Representatives, I'm curious to know what factors you think are critical to building influence.

There are three things that I think go hand-in-hand with influence, especially regarding politics: trust, collaboration, and flexibility. In my experience, the trust component comes from two things: relationships, which enable people to trust your intuition, and demonstrated content knowledge. For example, my background is in economic development. When I became an elected official, that background lent me credibility in speaking about issues related to job growth because that's what I'd spent my academic life and my professional life working on.

Can you expand on what you mean by collaboration as necessary for influence?

You can't expect people to be there for the landing if they aren't there for the takeoff. You have to seek input. You might have experience doing this without realizing it; personally, I think some of my influencing skills came from being the youngest of three brothers. I would've never gotten my way on anything unless I could convince at least one of my brothers to come to my way of thinking.

Persuading enough people to support your position to move things forward is the nature of the legislative process. Serving in the state legislature and now in Congress has helped me learn how to bring people around to my way of thinking. If I'm going to be maximally influential, I have to get buy-in from those I'm trying to influence. That takes collaboration.

I think many of us have trouble picturing any collaboration going on in Congress these days. Can you share an example of this collaboration producing results?

One of the things I've been proudest of in my congressional career is my involvement in the creation of the Olympic Forest Collaborative. There's a long history of controversy regarding forest management in our region. When I took office, the dynamic was pretty disheartening. The timber industry felt like the status quo wasn't working for them and was damaging the economies of local communities. The conservation community felt like the status quo wasn't working for them either—that forest practices weren't good for forest health. We tried to get all the parties into the same room to figure out a path that worked better for everybody.

Initially, getting both sides to sit down together and talk productively was quite difficult. Their primary interactions for decades had been in courtrooms. For the first six months or so, it was an exercise in trying to keep people in the room so they could share their agendas and their priorities. We took some field trips to build trust and give folks an opportunity to listen to each other. A little while later, we started pulling together some projects that addressed needs on both sides of the table. We identified some ecological thinning projects that provided economic opportunity for the local timber industry but that also contributed positively to forest health. And now, a few years in, we've seen a significant increase in harvest levels and zero litigation from the environmental community, because they are able to weigh in with ideas and concerns on the front end.

It's refreshing to hear about collaboration leading to influential decisions, especially in our current political climate. In your personal experience, how often do you see this sort of influence tactic at work?

I'm glad to say that I see it quite frequently. I can give you a great example from the Bipartisan Working Group in Congress, which I currently chair. A dozen Democrats and a dozen Republicans meet for breakfast every week. To start, we talk about what we're working on and, if possible, we invite collaboration and co-sponsorship. Next we talk about what's going on in Congress. Those can be feisty conversations, but I'm increasingly of the belief that good democracy is a little bit like a good marriage. You don't necessarily agree with your partner on everything, but you've got to be able to listen as well as talk, and to not impugn each other's motives. In politics, differing perspectives can often turn into *the Jerry Springer Show*. So we spend some time trying to get a better understanding of where people are coming from.

"If you've influenced someone, you've convinced them to do something you wanted, but that doesn't mean they're doing it for the reasons you want them to."

In the last part of the meeting we talk about big, hairy issues facing the country and try to figure out where we can find some common ground and move forward. It's not like we hold hands around the table and sing "Kumbaya" or close our eyes and do trust falls into each other's arms. But it's been a powerful way to dial down the toxicity and build some relationships.

This sort of collaboration really does lead to progress. Once we invited an expert on campaign finance reform, Trevor Potter, to present to the group. Trevor had been the attorney for John McCain's presidential campaign and a Republican appointee to the Federal Election Commission. He talked to us about some of the dysfunction behind a failure to enforce campaign finance law in recent years. I said, "I'd like to work on fixing that."

Because of the relationships I'd developed—which go back to the trust component—some of my Republican colleagues said, "We'll work with you on that." And we wrote a bill together and introduced it together. That bill was the first bipartisan campaign finance reform bill introduced in more than a decade. It's an influential piece of legislation, and it was only possible because we worked together.

How does this all tie in to the third component of influence you mentioned: flexibility?

Collaboration implies a certain level of flexibility, of course, but I think it's important to call it out on its own. If you've influenced someone, you've convinced them to do something you wanted, but that doesn't mean they're doing it for the reasons you want them to—and that's okay. Sometimes we can come from entirely different directions and yet reach the same conclusion.

For example, when I started in the US House, I sponsored a bill that was focused on helping asset-poor people save money. The work was based on the research of a Harvard economist who found that asset-poor people disproportionately *don't* save money and disproportionately *do* play the lottery. This economist found that by linking the excitement of gambling to the act of saving rather than spending, you could help people save a lot of money. In a nutshell, each time someone deposited twenty-five dollars, they would earn an entry into a drawing for a cash prize. A person's deposit was never at risk, so the worst that could happen was that someone saved money.

I approached one of my Republican colleagues in hopes of having him cosponsor my bill. I explained the proposal and the rationale behind it. After a long pause, he said to me, "So, what you're talking about is eliminating onerous regulations that prohibit financial institutions from offering innovative products that make people more self-sufficient and less reliant on government." After another long pause, I responded, "Sure."

For me, it was about helping poor people save money. For my colleague, it was about something entirely different. But the point is, I managed to bring him to the same conclusion. I had to be comfortable with the fact that we got there in different ways. We were both flexible.

So you're saying it's better to judge influence by the outcome, not the motivation behind it.

Right. Being flexible doesn't mean you abandon your goal. I was always impressed by my state's former governor, Chris Gregoire, who was extremely goal-oriented. She was kind and good at building relationships, but when she wanted to get something across the finish line she used the power of her office to get it there...sometimes literally. There are lots of stories of people being locked in Governor Gregoire's office during a stalemate. She would let everyone make their case, blow the whistle if someone was being unreasonable, and make it clear that folks weren't leaving the room until there was an agreement.

Do you strive to teach others how to influence behavior more effectively? If so, what factors make one person a more adept learner than others?

I've learned so much from leaders like Governor Gregoire and countless others, and I do strive to pay that education forward. As chair of the New Democrat Coalition, for instance, I mentor some of our new members. Congress isn't exactly a legislative juggernaut these days. You don't get many shots on goal. Helping others identify and make those shots, helping them be more effective, is really satisfying. The most adept learners have a strong appetite for feedback and coaching, and honestly, most new representatives share those qualities. After all, most people aren't in Congress because we want to be something—we're in Congress because we want to do something.

If we were to give you a billboard that millions of people could see, what would you say about influence?

Being flexible doesn't mean you abandon your goal.

EDITOR'S NOTES

Collaboration is the key to being effective in any domain, as Michael Armstrong and Will Hurd also demonstrate.

"Being flexible doesn't mean you abandon your goal."

—Derek Kilmer

“When you’re not looking for accolades and you’re just looking to get things done, it’s amazing what you can accomplish.”

Michael D. Armstrong is executive vice president, worldwide television licensing and operations, at Paramount Pictures. Previously, he served BET Networks as general manager and Viacom International Media Networks as executive vice president and general manager, revenue and emerging brands

Armstrong has led many firsts for Paramount, including the creation and international launch of Paramount Channel, now the largest ad-supported film channel in the world. Armstrong co-led the launch of BET Play and has been instrumental in growing Spike’s distribution internationally.

Armstrong received a BS in marketing from Hampton University, where he also serves on the board, and an MBA from the University of Chicago Booth School of Business. He is the immediate past chair for the NAMIC (National Association for Multi-Ethnicity in Communications) Board of Directors; chairman of the board for the Dance Theatre of Harlem; and on the board of directors for Public Radio International.

Show up with Trust and Kindness

Michael D. Armstrong

Based on your life experience and your profession, how do you define the word influence?

Influence is essentially getting people to follow you. Now, how do you get people to do that? How do you get people to believe in the things that are core to your values and your belief system? You have to build trust. And you build trust by doing what you say you're going to do, by being a person of high integrity, and by respecting others. That means being respectful of their time and listening to them—in most cases, listening more than you talk. A big part of showing someone that you respect them is being able to feed them back answers that show that you heard what they were saying.

Any time you're trying to influence someone to take action, whether that's transacting a multi-million dollar business deal or getting your kids to clean their room, there's one core question: What's in it for that person on the other end? You have to prove that, by doing what you're asking them to do, they'll be solving something in their life or doing something that they can feel good about. Personally and professionally, getting to that point always involves the same factors: trust, respect, integrity, and just showing up the same way each and every time.

In thinking about those factors that define influence for you, how deliberate have you been in developing them? What's your mental model?

My approach to life is honestly grounded in watching how my parents lived their lives. I love that my mom and dad were kind to people. They were open and honest in their approach.

They were both entrepreneurs. I happened to follow my mother into her profession—she worked twenty-five years in the cable television industry. My father was a CPA with his own accounting firm. During my formative years, I got to see how they approached the ups and downs of entrepreneurship—they would talk openly and honestly with us about the things that were going on in their lives. I learned through the pattern of watching my parents live a really fruitful life. And now I get to enjoy them in their retirement, living a couple hours from me. It's a great thing to let them see how their parenting brought about what they always dreamed of for my siblings and me.

I would love an example or two of how you have built influence. Where did you learn a positive lesson about implementing these factors and seeing the resulting influence?

I've had a really great career at Viacom, most of which has involved doing things that I would consider intrapreneurship. I love the concept of the intrapreneur versus the entrepreneur: you can do entrepreneurial things inside of an organization and get the same benefits of building something from scratch and working with teams. Where I really had to build influence was around getting people in other markets around the globe to work toward a common goal—in my case, launching and building networks outside of the United States in markets where I didn't speak the language but my local colleagues did.

I may not have known the dynamics of a given market, but I was the leader of the overall brand, and I was charged with shepherding the adoption of the brand by colleagues who reported to people other than myself. The best example is when we built out the Paramount Channel in 2012. I was asked to launch a movie network in partnership with our Paramount Pictures group, where I happen to work now, but at the time I was on the Viacom International Media Networks team.

We were not first to market with a film channel, and we certainly were not Paramount's only internal customer. My approach was to build trust that we were going to do something different, and the channel was going to drive growth for the local business. We were going to honor the value of the Paramount brand, which was turning one hundred. I had to make sure that lawyers at the studio understood how I was going to utilize the brand while convincing people in local markets why they needed to add yet another channel to their portfolios. And I had to convince our clients and advertisers to trust that this was the best place to display their products and services to reach a new audience.

We did all that with great success. I think it's because, as the brand lead, I was able to influence everybody to see the launch as an historic event. No one had ever launched a channel that was dedicated to who we were as a brand. To get people all over the globe to have their own Paramount Channel, from Russia to Hungary to Spain to

Asia, required influencing a lot of people along the value chain.

It was an incredible honor to have the opportunity to do that. It gave me a chance to sharpen my skills since I was dealing with cultures that varied market to market, from both client and internal colleague perspectives. It was all about building trust on a local level that this kid from Colorado, living in New York, could focus in on what mattered market by market—and give each one enough flexibility to make sure their market would be successful while preserving the integrity and consistency of the Paramount brand.

A global effort like this raises a question about your approach to communication. How did you go about establishing your credibility with all these different parties?

The key was making sure to give enough time and resources to meet each market on its own terms. If you're dealing with someone in Asia, you take the late-night calls and make sure that you're not just inconveniencing your colleagues. Learning the greetings in each local language goes such a long way. It shows them that you are taking that extra effort to respect them and their culture, which leads them to receive you in a different way. Likewise, it's important to spend time with your colleagues outside of work, enjoying the local customs and foods and building friendships.

I have some of the greatest friends from my twenty-plus years at Viacom, and it's that friendship and respect that allows one to get things done in a much quicker way. If I need to move the business forward in a certain way, I have people all around the company I can call on. It's important to maintain connection and pay attention to the little things. Make sure you understand people and what drives them and their passion.

Maintaining connection doesn't have to be a huge effort. I recently forwarded an article to a friend of mine about the fonts chosen for an election and what those connote about the candidates; he works for a big company that manages campaigns. It was my way of staying on his radar by saying, "Hey, I know what's important to you. I thought you might like this article." I do a lot of that, connecting with people in a way that's more than just transactional.

Who's been really influential for you on your path to where you are today? What did you learn from them?

Well, I've already talked a bit about my parents. Another key person in my life is my wife. Most people would say, "Oh, she's your biggest cheerleader," but actually she's not at all a cheerleader. She's my best coach. It's not just about raising me up and rah-rah-ing me when things are going great. She also challenges me to do better and to give more. And many of the opportunities that I've had professionally in my life came about because my wife knew that I could do more and encouraged me to do so.

Professionally, I've had so many people along the way who have been great influences on me. One of the first was Tom Freston, who was the president of MTV Networks when I first encountered him. When I moved to New York in 2002, I had a chance to spend a lot of time with him through Viacom's structured mentorship program. He dispensed phenomenal advice, talking to me about his early years working in the company and the triumphs and mistakes that he made. He allowed me to be open and honest with him about where I was at any given point in my career.

I've also had the benefit of working very closely with our current CEO, Bob Bakish. I worked for him when he was running international and I was launching Paramount Channel, Spike, and BET. Watching him, I learned how to set a strategy and a path for our new initiatives and ensure that all our resources were focused on getting us there.

One other person who was incredibly influential to me was Debra Lee, chairman and CEO of BET Networks. She took a chance on me to do something critical to her success and legacy, which was to launch the business outside the United States. She gave me a chance to lead BET into the international sphere, knowing I had never launched a channel and had barely done any business outside the United States other than ad sales. She let me take the reins and gave me the chance to make key decisions, tolerating the mistakes I made along the way.

I really appreciated that Debra gave me the opportunity to sit at the table with her other key executives. I learned so much. Now, I always encourage young executives to remember that, when you're at that table, you're there for a reason. What you contribute is a new perspective, and a new perspective tends to create breakthroughs. You deserve to be there.

Personally, I've also been deeply influenced by Dr. William Harvey. I had the pleasure of going to Hampton University, one of the nation's premier historically black colleges and universities, where he has served as president for forty-two years. I now have the distinct pleasure of serving closely with him as a member of the board of trustees. He exemplifies what it means to be a leader, what it means to be influential, and what it means to draw people into your vision, to show them the value your organization can create for its members. One of his former vice presidents now runs the University of the Bahamas. In the wake of Hurricane Dorian, which devastated the island, Dr. Harvey reached out to him and asked, "How can we help? How can we be of service?" Now Hampton is going to take in and pay for students who were displaced by the storm—room, board, transportation, and tuition for a semester for as many students as can make it. That way, they won't have an interruption in their studies.

This kind of thing is how true leaders, influencers in this world, show up in times of need. It sets an example that up-and-coming leaders want to follow.

“When you’re at that table, you’re there for a reason. What you contribute is a new perspective, and a new perspective tends to create breakthroughs. You deserve to be there.”

As you think about younger folks who aspire to be executives at your level, what advice would you give? Take a newly minted MBA who has all the smarts to do the job but maybe hasn't figured out how to navigate the people and the relationship side.

I meet with people all the time because I feel it's my honor and privilege to be where I am. I see it as my duty to give back to others by sharing what I know. I tend to tell newly minted MBAs or undergrads in their first jobs the same thing: You have something unique to give. Whether or not you understand this industry, you understand your position in a way that other colleagues around the table don't.

Most of the people I'm talking to right now are either Generation Z or Millennials. They live each and every day of their lives understanding what it's like to be the consumer. When they come into the room in front of people like myself, with gray hair in their beards, we don't want them to leave their personal sides at the door. They have something valuable to contribute because their experience and their perspective is different.

I think about that as an African American male. I bring a perspective into a room of colleagues, fellow executives, and clients that speaks from the point of view of someone who has spent forty-seven years on this Earth as a black man. Most of them cannot bring that to the table. They can bring their own experiences to the table, and I hope they do. But I can contribute a fulsome conversation based on my own experiences and how those experiences can inform our decisions on a particular strategy. That's really important. We have a diverse and inclusive organization, and everybody has the opportunity to bring their full self to work.

You sent me a movie recommendation: *The Black Godfather.* Can you talk about some lessons from that movie that are applicable to the conversation we're having?

The Black Godfather is a documentary by a colleague and friend of mine, Reggie Hudlin, who's done a lot of work with Viacom and used to work at BET as head of programming. It's about a really influential person named Clarence Avant, a guy from rural North Carolina who came to Hollywood and found a way to use what he had as a person, based on how he'd seen his parents and friends and everyone around him operate, to get things done. He applied that to business. He was just there for his clients in a way that they had never seen someone show up. He was loyal. He understood that it was important to be there for people in their time of need. And when it came time for him to have someone stand up for him in his time of need, people showed up in a big way.

That documentary touched me in a lot of different ways. One, Clarence had no bounds about what he could do. He was asked to create soundtracks for movies. He had never done it, but he worked with a client, and next thing you know, he was executive producer for all of these wonderful compositions for some of the biggest films of the time.

The film really captured that you don't have to go to the best school. You don't have to go through all of the best training. You have to be a person who's going to bring it all each and every day, and you draw on the things that you know have been successful for you in your life. You have to make sure your word is your bond. Clarence became this massive figure behind the scenes because he didn't care about the spotlight. When you're not looking for accolades and you're just looking to get things done, it's amazing what you can accomplish.

If you could have a billboard with an important message about influence that millions of people would see everyday, what would you want it to say?

You know, I go back to this kind of simple message that I believe encapsulates what it means to influence people: Be nice.

And why do I say that that's important? You disarm people when you show up in a way that's warm, that is inviting. I have found that in business, people want to do business with people they like. It doesn't matter who you're dealing with; there's no reason at any juncture, in any interaction with anybody, anywhere in the world, that you shouldn't show up with a smile on your face and open arms, willing to have a conversation. Bring your best self, and disarm people with kindness.

EDITOR'S NOTES

Like Ethan Burris, Dianna Kokoszka and Vanessa Bohns, Armstrong encourages people to find and use the influence they already have.

"Bring your best self, and disarm people with kindness."

—Michael D. Armstrong

“Influence is one of the essential, identifying marks of a true, successful leader.”

Dianna Kokoszka's real estate career began in record fashion with 104 home sales in her first year—and more than 4,000 since. She owned her own real estate company before joining Keller Williams, where she became the CEO and President of M.A.P.S., a coaching program that under her leadership earned a place in Training magazine's Hall of Fame. The program also earned a Stevie Award as Sales Training and Coaching Program of the Year and a Prism Award for outstanding organizational coaching, and helped establish Keller Williams Realty as the number one training company in the world.

Within Keller Williams, Dianna earned the Award of Excellence (2010) and the Robert B. “Bob” Carter Inspiration Award (2016). She was among the 2016 Swanepoel 200 list of the most powerful leaders in residential real estate, and among Inman News' top 25 coaches in the industry.

Dianna is a John Maxwell-certified coach and author of nineteen books on running a real estate business. She enjoys waterskiing, traveling, reading, and spending time with her children and grandchildren. She and her husband Tony DiCello live in Austin, Texas.

To Be Influential, Be Intentional

Dianna Kokoszka

How do you define influence? What does it mean to you?

At its core, influence is about making people move. Our actions and inaction, our displayed and private emotions, our spoken words and silences, can all change the trajectories of other peoples' lives. Our power to move others is both awesome and ominous. Not only can we do this, we can't stop ourselves from doing this. In one way or another, knowingly or unknowingly, we are always exerting influence on the people around us.

So, the question is not *whether* we will influence people, it's *how* we will. What direction will we move them in, and how far? How intentional will we be about it? Sometimes we move people by blazing a trail and "boldly going where no one has gone before." People see that we are going somewhere with determination, and they are drawn into the journey with us. They may not know exactly where we are headed or see as far as we are seeing—and yet there is still something irresistibly magnetic that pulls them in.

This sort of influence can be very intentional, and yet it often isn't. Either way, it can be quite transformational for people. While people might start out moving along with us, attached to our vision, in time they take on the vision themselves. When they take ownership of it, even modifying it to make it their own, then we know we've truly influenced them.

We can also influence others by helping them gain clarity around and move toward their own dreams rather than by enlisting them in our missions. In this case, it's more about standing beside them or behind them, helping them move out of their comfort zones, out of a nest that might otherwise have become a prison if we or someone else hadn't come along. Whether it's by leading them or launching them, influence is about delivering people from their own inertia.

Seen from this perspective, influence is one of the essential, identifying marks of a true, successful leader. It's not about title or position. Plenty of people have titles yet lack true, lasting influence. Leaders move the people around them in significant ways. One of my mentors is John Maxwell, whose expertise is in organizational leadership. He says that leadership is influence, nothing more and nothing less. Some leaders may have purely organizational influence, moving people because of the company's structure and hierarchy. When people follow only due to the consequences for not following, that's not true leadership.

Real, transformational leaders influence others from the inside out, not the outside in. People respond to them not because they have to, because they want to. They almost can't help themselves. Look inside any effective organization, and you'll see individuals without formal roles and titles who are nevertheless highly influential.

What factors do you think drive influence?

You have to be committed to both contribution and connection. Every day at 7:00 a.m. the alarm on my phone goes off with a notification that asks, "What will you do to add value to other people today?" Every night at 7:00 p.m., another notification asks, "What did you do to add value to other people today?"

Those alarms are in my phone because one of my core values is a commitment to "coming from contribution." When we intentionally and programmatically think about how we can add value to the people in our world, and then actually carry it out, we are modeling a way of being even as we are carrying out our own commitment to serve others.

"Coming from contribution" implies the necessity of developing the skill of connection. Connection is about the intentional pursuit of and engagement with the people in our world. It is about moving with confidence toward others. It is about being authentic—being who we really are, where we are, all the time. And it is about continually choosing to be other-centered, to focus on the one before you, to be more interested in listening than speaking. It's about suspending judgment and staying in curiosity. When we value coming from contribution and practice this sort of connection, the impact and influence that result from that are multiplied exponentially.

If you're going to have influence over anyone else, first you have to know who you are, where you're going, and why.

There are two critical dates in life. The day you are born and the day you find out why—when you figure out what it is you are uniquely here for. This "big why" is typically a reflection of your strengths,

“Real, transformational leaders influence others from the inside out, not the outside in.”

experiences, deepest values, hopes, convictions, and most significant relationships. Your "big why" is the thing that gets you out of bed in the morning. It is what enables you to live a life by design as opposed to a life that you just stumble through by default.

Knowing why you're here and, accordingly, where you're going, is what adds weight and substance to life and makes the influence you bring to bear on others so powerful. Others can borrow the force that drives you for a while and use it to better understand their own "big why" and move purposefully outward from there.

In the movie *Forrest Gump*, there's a scene where Forrest goes out for a jog and then keeps running. What began as a random decision becomes an obsession. Soon countless others are fascinated by his mysterious choice and join him. It becomes a national craze until at one point, in the middle of nowhere, with a train of others running behind him, he simply stops. Without a word of explanation, he turns and heads home. The people following him are confused and don't know what it means. And that is the point: Forrest wasn't going anywhere in particular—he was just going. And the people following him were certainly influenced, yet not in a meaningful way. To have significant and lasting influence, you need to know where you're going and why.

When did you discover your "big why"?

I started working at age five in my mom and dad's grocery store. By the time I was nine, I had learned

"There are two critical dates in life. The day you are born and the day you find out why."

to stock shelves, sweep floors, stock produce, and run the cash register. Doing different jobs allowed me to realize that it wasn't about the money—even though I loved making money. My parents also taught me that when you learn something, if you share it with others you will become better at it yourself. My mother taught me to twirl a baton, and I immediately started teaching other girls to twirl a baton. It hit me one day that I was here to help people learn. I became a teacher at heart. I found myself working in the store and teaching dance and baton, all because I loved helping others. The statement "Do what you love, and the money will show up" has been true for me.

After reading Michael Gerbers' book *The E-Myth Revisited*, I found out he was offering a consultant's certification program. There were eight of us chosen to be in his class. The first day he asked us to write our own eulogies. The more I worked on mine, the more I looked at it and thought, "Uh, that sounds so egotistical." That caused me to rewrite it over and over again, being more concise with each draft. At about two in the morning, the memories of the dance and twirling class came back to me, and I thought, "Yeah, I'm here to make a positive difference in people's lives."

What transpired from this exercise is that I found my purpose—I strive to be remembered this way: "She made a positive difference." It's not just about getting someone to change. Change is temporary. I desire something bigger than that. I'm after transformation. I want the people and organizations that I influence to change from the inside out, to transform into something greater than they could have ever imagined on their own.

I love your example of intention and the 7:00 a.m. alarm as a habit-building nudge. What other mechanisms help with establishing influence and intention?

Commit yourself to being a lifetime learner. The idea behind this is simple, yet profound: your influence grows to the extent that you do. If you're always leaning forward and seeking clarity, depth of understanding, and insight, your perspectives will be continually challenged, shaped, and nuanced in healthy ways. Keeping that commitment means you'll never stagnate. Continually investing in yourself in this way will add a depth and maturity to your understanding that there are no shortcuts for and that only time on task can produce.

As the old saying goes, if the only tool in your toolbox is a hammer, you will tend to treat everything like a nail. A commitment to lifelong learning increases the likelihood of you being the person who—at the right time and in the right place and in the right way—pulls out the tool that becomes the catalyst for significant change in someone else's life. Also, be intentional about what you are thinking, what you are feeling, and what you are doing every day. Each of these things emanates energy. We know from physics that energy cannot be created or destroyed, only transferred or transformed. Be aware of your energy and how it influences others, positively or negatively. Since we live largely in a cause-and-effect world, the quality of our energy will determine the scope of our influence.

As I said earlier, while you do not need a title to be a leader and have influence, you must have intention. Princess Diana is actually a great example of this. She was a commoner who married royalty, and she turned that into an identity that helped her connect with people. Even though she represented the royal family, she made it her goal to serve others. In that process, she built relationships. Her influence kept increasing, which gave her the ability to make things happen. Diana knew who she wanted to be, she was of service to others, and she took a stand. All of these things gave her influence.

Knowing your big why, commitment to contribution and connection, and the pursuit of lifetime learning are some of the most significant factors and the best predictors of how much influence one can have on the lives of others.

I'd like to switch gears and ask you for some advice. Let's say I'm a young real estate agent, and I want to build a successful career. What advice would you give me? What would you tell me to do?

One of the first things I would say comes from John Maxwell. He was the one that introduced me to the "Rule of Five." He asked me, "If every day you took an axe and swung it at the same tree, what would eventually happen to the tree?" "Well," I said, "It would fall over." He then asked, "What if you took a baseball bat and hit the tree five times every day? Would it fall over then?" It wouldn't, of course. He then likened my goals to that tree and the axe. He said, "Find the five things you must do every day to make your goal a reality." Attach the right skills or tools (the axe, not the bat) to those five things, and you will reach success. Those words got me thinking and, before long, I had developed my rule of five for selling.

When I committed myself to doing—and then actually did—these five things every work day, I found massive success. Every day I would lead generate, lead follow-up, go on appointments, negotiate contracts, and role-play my scripts, dialogs, objection handlers, and presentations.

So, my advice to a young real estate professional would be to do those five things every day, Monday through Friday. My business grew exponentially, and so will yours!

A second piece of advice I would give is this: 90 percent of your success has to do with mindset. The things you tell yourself have the greatest impact on what you believe is and is not possible, and those will determine whether or not you will break through the artificial limitations you place on yourself. I was given an opportunity by Keller Williams to create an entire training program around this reality, which I named BOLD: Business Objective, a Life by Design. The men and women who took the program to heart and implemented its principles became successful with mathematical precision.

A third piece of advice I would give to a young real estate agent is this: be intentional. Intentionality is within everyone's reach. You can do it starting right now. Design the life you choose to live. Too many people are living a life by default, allowing others to write their stories for them. Stop giving the pen to other people. Once you start living intentionally and take responsibility for your own story, you will find yourself gaining more confidence and a surprising side benefit: joy. Joy comes from finding alignment between who you are and where you are going. Influence will grow in surprising ways that flow out of the intentionality, confidence, and joy that define your life.

I'm going to give you a billboard, and millions of people will see it every day. What do you want it to say about influence?

Who are you influencing? Make it count.

EDITOR'S NOTES

Like all the contributors to this book, Kokoszka makes what she does look easy. Her interview and many others remind us that true influence takes strategy, planning, and persistent effort over time; there are no shortcuts.

"Who are you influencing? Make it count."

—Dianna Kokoszka

"Connecting with others is finding our shared internal struggles. It's finding the humanity of my voice."

Vince Kadlubek is cofounder and CEO of Meow Wolf, an art collective that has transformed into an award-winning arts production company. After leading Meow Wolf to win the inaugural competition from Creative Startups, Vince created the business plan for the collective's House of Eternal Return, the Santa Fe art experience that catapulted the collective to fame. He has continued as a force of vision for the company, subverting current business paradigms while building reliable systems to bring transformative, immersive art experiences to the world. New Meow Wolf exhibitions are coming to Las Vegas, Denver, Washington D.C., and Phoenix.

Connecting Thought, Humanity, and Voice

Vince Kadlubek

What determines whether or not someone is an influencer?

To be influential means you set trends; people look to you for direction. A lot of futurists aren't necessarily influencers, though. Influencers stand on the precipice of what is going to be. If you're too far past it, or not close enough to it, then you're not going to be an influencer. You have to be anchored close to the edge of what's to come.

Have you been conscious about building your influence, or has it just happened?

I've been conscious about it. I know my voice. I know that who I am internally and what I project externally are seamless: I am my own billboard. I've been very conscious in developing a relationship between my thoughts and my words, connecting both to who I actually am. That ensures authenticity as well as vulnerability. I've made intentional decisions around how I use my voice not to just

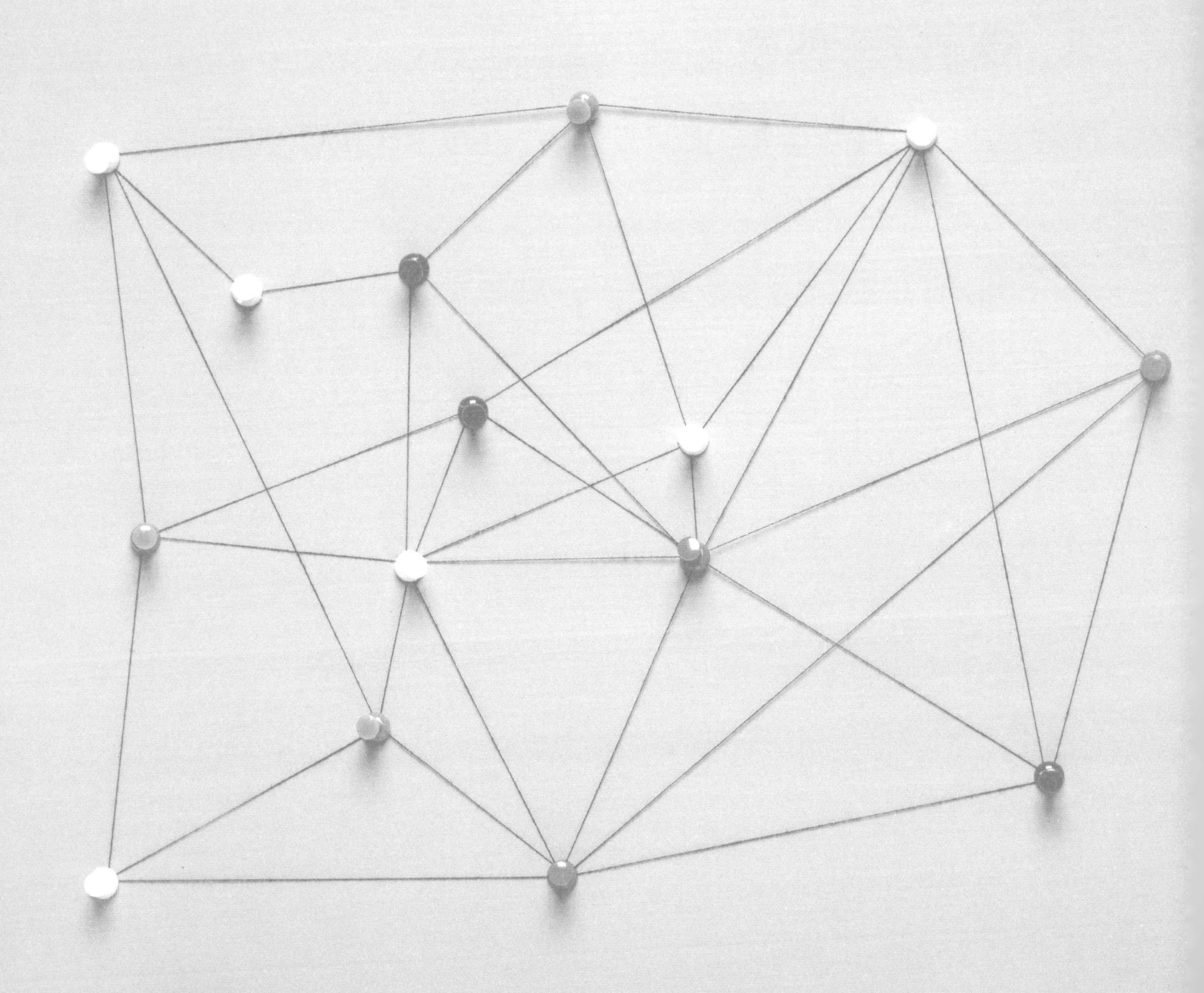

project what's lofty, ambitious, and visionary, but also to express the small, the minute, the human flaws.

Ultimately, my influence will be greater when my voice is trusted, and my voice can only be trusted if it connects with others. And connecting with others is finding our shared internal struggles. It's finding the humanity of my voice.

I've also been very intentional about tapping into existing trends, finding what's wrong with them, and calling it out. Take intellectual property regeneration, where studios go to the same well over and over again for films. Like, "*Star Wars* is so popular right now, let's keep delivering yet more *Star Wars*." When I started objecting to this two years ago, it wasn't quite yet the trendy thing to say. What was trendy was, "Yes, more *Star Wars*." When something seems to be at peak popularity, it's most likely on the verge of being disrupted. To be influential, it's key to understand the logical next step of that disruption.

So I'm a new father, and I think a lot about how kids love familiarity and predictability. Part of what you're saying is yes, that's true, but we all love discovery, too. How would you think about the blend of those two with respect to influencing people's minds and behavior?

Once you develop a predictable foundation and structure, you are free to explore the unknown. It's in that space that you can introduce unpredictability

"Once you develop a predictable foundation and structure, you are free to explore the unknown."

and spontaneity and where influence can be really strong. Can I develop a predictable, familiar, connected base and then—and *then*—go and venture into the unknown and bring people along with me?

The base of predictability and familiarity lies in some of those qualities that I was just talking about: me as the leader expressing vulnerability, expressing human qualities. Then in my organizational structure and social structure, there are a lot of things that need to happen in order to continue building that base of familiarity. We need office space, we need office hours, we need HR, we need a lot of predictable things in order for the company to feel comfortable enough to venture into the unknown. You constantly have to balance the predictable with the unpredictable.

Who's shown you this path, or who do you really look up to?

I think that golden-era Apple was inspiring in that you never knew what they were going to do next. Innovation was the core of their company. And in general, the immersive design community—the movement itself—has been huge in terms of establishing some sense of reality and then venturing into the fiction. Interestingly, Obama was probably a big influence there. It was like, how can one connect at a human level and then also express this soaring, huge idealism?

Here's a question I'm excited to ask you. A lot of us from the outside look at someone with creative influence and assume it's a gift, that it happens really naturally for somebody. Can you talk to me about how hard you work at it? How much of this just really comes naturally and is part of the fabric of what you do, and how much of it is deliberate and practiced?

I feel like I've worked really hard at it, and now it comes across as natural just because it's a skill that I've developed. It's a skill of understanding spontaneity in every moment so that when I talk, it doesn't sound like I am scripted. When people say, "You sound so authentic, and you're such a clear communicator," it's because I'm searching for the words as I'm saying them and I also have a good way of being able to pattern my voice and my language in a way that is familiar to people. I'm not just shooting off every spontaneous thought. I've worked incredibly hard on developing the actual connection between thought and voice. It's all about effective communication.

Music to my ears. What's the one piece of advice you have for me if I want to learn the skill of "prepared spontaneity"? Where should I start?

You have to realize that an identity has been developed that is prepackaging your thoughts before they turn into voice. I had to break down and dissolve that side of me, and I still have to constantly check on it, or else that identity will take over again. Break that identity down by getting out of the secondary voice and into the primary voice: be the voice that thinks, not the voice that's interpreting the thought. You *are* the thought; you're voicing the thought directly. We all have this internal dialogue that will filter what actually gets said. Dissolving that internal dialogue is critical to building a true connection between your thoughts and your voice.

All right. One more thing. I'm going to give you a billboard that millions of people are going to drive by every day. What would you have it say about influence?

There's a statement that I like a lot involving individuals, but I think it works collectively, too. For individuals, the statement would be, "You are not who you have been. You are who you are becoming." Collectively, the billboard could read,

"We are not who we have been. We are who we are becoming."

That's the core of influence, to me: realizing that our identity is based not on what we've become comfortable with in the past but on the choices we make into the future.

EDITOR'S NOTES

Authenticity is another recurring theme in this book, as many contributors remind us that, while we should tailor our delivery based on our audiences, we need to ensure the message itself is consistent if we want to be influential.

"We are not who we have been. We are who we are becoming."

—Vince Kadlubek

“There are a lot of ways to influence people’s behaviors so they think they’re doing things out of their own volition, but they’re really being unconsciously manipulated by stimuli in their environment.”

Dr. Heather Berlin is a cognitive neuroscientist, professor of psychiatry at the Icahn School of Medicine at Mount Sinai, and a visiting scholar at the New York Psychoanalytic Society and Institute.

Passionate about science communication and promoting women in STEM, Berlin is a committee member of the National Academy of Sciences’ Science and Entertainment Exchange and a member of the American Association for the Advancement of Science’s Committee on Science and Technology Engagement with the Public.

She hosts *Startalk All-Stars* with Neil DeGrasse Tyson and has hosted series on PBS and the Discovery Channel. Dr. Berlin cowrote and stars in the off-Broadway production *Off the Top*, about the neuroscience of improvisation, and she premiered her comedy about the brain basis of desire, *Impulse Control*, at the 2019 Edinburgh Fringe Festival. Her numerous media appearances include the BBC, *National Geographic*, TEDx, and the documentary *Bill Nye: Science Guy*.

Influence and the Unconscious

Heather Berlin

Based on your view of the world and your neuroscience background, how do you define the word influence?

Influence is when someone or something has an effect, either positive or negative, on someone else's thoughts, feelings, or behavior. It doesn't even have to be humans—the sun can have an influence on which direction a plant grows. But in the realm of people, influence makes us think, feel, or behave in a way we would not have otherwise.

There are many factors that go into determining why and how much people can be influenced, many of which come down to psychology. For instance, suggestibility, or how readily a person will take on a suggestion, or how that person will respond to perceived authority. There's a "white coat" phenomenon where people are more likely to trust and be influenced by someone wearing a white coat; people think, "Okay, this is the doctor, the scientist, the one who knows the information—I'd better listen."

A lot of people who are easily influenced are looking for answers or aren't sure what direction to go in their life, and they seek guidance from people they admire or think are authority figures. This puts the influencer in the position of having to be careful with their degree of influence. With great power comes great responsibility, right? You have to be aware of your influence and how it will affect other people.

The thing to remember is, all of us are being unconsciously influenced by our environments all of the time. The unconscious processing capacity of the brain is vastly greater than the conscious processing capacity, and only a small subset of the information processed by the unconscious brain becomes available to our conscious minds. So a big part of cognitive psychology and neuroscience is working out and measuring the ways our behavior is influenced by things we are unaware of and what is happening in the brain when those influences occur.

In a way, you can think of influential people as those who have figured out, consciously or unconsciously, how to navigate the brain's natural heuristic "shortcuts" to taking on information. Everything around the brain is vastly more complex than it can track, so the brain has evolved to simplify information in ways that are useful, if not necessarily accurate. Influencers find ways to get "taken in" by the brains of their audience via side routes, like the Khaleesi conquering the city of Mereen in *Game of Thrones*, not by smashing down the gates but by sending soldiers to sneak in through the sewer system. The more you learn about the brain, the better you can fortify your city!

What do you think drives people to want to be influential?

Some people, I think, are just influential without being motivated to be so; they are simply doing what they enjoy doing or what they're good at, and that has an effect on other people. For example, take Einstein studying physics. He was doing it because he wanted to understand the laws of the universe, and he inadvertently influenced the work of many other people.

But there are other people who set out to influence others, whether they're in politics and want to make a change in the world or they crave fame and popularity. I've been really interested in that. What's happening in their brains? Why do some people seek out fame? It turns out that the markers of popularity, such as getting likes or follows online, activate the reward networks in the brain. Pursuing fame can be addictive. These people want to be influential because it makes them feel good.

It makes you wonder what separates the people we view as "attention seekers" from the people we view as more genuine, when really we all want to be authentic and we all want to follow our passion. But we often go to great lengths to protect our egos. How much are we willing to share about our own selfish desires to be famous? How much do we hide, even from ourselves? For some people, this can lead them to lie to themselves.

Even dictators don't have a narrative of "I'm doing this for power" or "I'm evil." They have some other story that they tell themselves to protect their egos. I imagine that Hitler had a narrative in his mind that he was doing the right thing for the world. It's hard to distinguish our true motives from the stories we tell ourselves, much less reveal the truth to other people.

Would it be authentic or ok to say out loud, "I want to be famous, I want to be an influencer"?

Sometimes we applaud people who just come out and say the honest truth even though it's ugly. Right? Like, if someone says, "Yeah, I just want to be famous. I just want to do stuff that's going to provoke people and get more followers," we can almost respect that honesty. But there are certainly many other people who won't admit they're driven by this motivation; they'll create some other narrative for themselves about what they're doing.

Kim Kardashian is an interesting case study. What is she famous for, really? Her looks? Maybe she was telling herself a grander story in the early days than, "I'm just trying to be famous for fame's sake," and maybe she wasn't, but now her narrative is that she's doing important things for the world. For example, she went to talk to Trump about prison reform, and now she's working toward becoming a lawyer and criminal justice advocate. There are people who become famous for other reasons and then try to use their powers for good and actually exert a positive influence.

How have you gained influence? What do you feel like your path has been to building the career platform you have?

I'm in that category of doing things that I'm passionate about, which may lead to me having influence in a certain area, but influence isn't my end goal. First and foremost, I'm passionate about understanding how the brain and mind work and helping develop more effective treatments for psychiatric and neurological disorders. But I also want to help people understand how their brains work and what motivates their behavior. In understanding the science, they may also be influenced by it and change their behavior accordingly or know themselves better.

For me, it's less about the messenger than the message, but I do realize that people are only going to care about the information if they care about who's delivering it. People are not going to absorb the information if I just stand there delivering boring talks about neuroscience. I try to get people excited about the information. I have a background in theater, which I think may have helped with my communication techniques. I was a fine arts and theater minor through college, and I acted in school plays from the time I was in kindergarten. I've always enjoyed getting up in front of audiences and connecting with people in that way, and all that theater experience came together for me in the realm of science communication.

But it wasn't an active process of seeking out influence over people. I just cared so much about this cool stuff that was going on in the lab and wanted to get other people who were not in my field excited about it.

You never really know how much of an influence you're having. It's so subjective. Even people I know who are objectively famous usually have a hard time gauging that. It's this weird dynamic where you have your own personal view of yourself and then this image that other people see. How to reconcile them is interesting and difficult.

Can you elaborate more on the importance of the message versus the delivery?

Most of my career has been as a basic scientist. In my field today, there are graduate students with their own blogs, and they're on Instagram, but when I was coming up, no one did that. You were just doing your science. That was it. There was no formal field of "science communication." Now you can get graduate degrees in it.

But I was just a scientist who was getting frustrated with putting in so much time and effort only to have the research go nowhere in the real world. You spend years writing and submitting grants, running research projects, and finally writing a paper, only to have to wait for the peer review and editorial process until it finally gets accepted. And then you have maybe a hundred people in your field who really care about it, and then it gets buried in some scientific journal somewhere, unless of course you discover the cure for cancer or some other Nobel Prize-worthy discovery.

Few people in the general public were hearing about the fascinating and important research happening in labs around the world. I started out just communicating my research results at science conferences among my colleagues, and I found that I really enjoyed that. Communicating the science and the findings for my peers transformed into doing it for more public audiences, and I really enjoyed that as well.

There are a lot of people who are good communicators but who are not experts in a scientific discipline. On the other hand, there are a lot of great scientific experts who are not good communicators. I was interested in how I could combine the two: doing really good science and communicating it effectively. Communication is a difficult skill to develop. It was important to me to keep working on it because I noticed that people cared more about the message when they connected with the person delivering it.

Can you share how you've developed that communication skill? What have you done?

One little trick that I've learned is how to focus your attention when you're in front of an audience. You should talk to the camera, or to one audience member at a time, like you're talking to your best friend—your best friend who's not an expert in the field, but whom you want to tell about some cool, new, exciting finding.

You try to break down the information in a way that is true to the science but doesn't contain a lot of the jargon. That's been one of the hardest things: you want to abstract it to avoid getting bogged down in the minutiae, but you also don't want to abstract it so much that it loses touch with the actual findings. For instance, you might say, "Okay, so we found activation in the amygdala—oh, the amygdala is a part of the brain involved in emotion."

You also have to try to make it exciting and meaningful to the person you're trying to communicate with. Storytelling is key; it's a great way to communicate. People remember stories. You can start with a personal story, then bleed into the science, and then come back around to something related to your story.

“You can think of influential people as those who have figured out, consciously or unconsciously, how to navigate the brain’s natural heuristic ‘shortcuts’ to taking on information.”

You're doing this fascinating work around impulses. How do you mesh the concept of impulses and influence? Is there a relationship between the two?

Most of what's happening in the brain is happening unconsciously, and it's influencing our behavior, which is why I've been focusing on unconscious processes. I'm doing a show now at the Edinburgh Fringe Festival, along with my husband Baba Brinkman, all about impulse control. We do an experiment every day with the audience where I have them make a decision, but we manipulate them: half the audience sees what we call an anchor—let's say a certain price for a product—and the other half of the audience sees a different anchor for the same product. They have to make a decision, and they're blatantly influenced by the anchor. It's just like some ads on TV. If you say, "These knives normally cost $19.99, but you can get them for just $7.99," it convinces people that they're getting a good deal even if the knives aren't actually worth more than five dollars. We can influence people with these framing effects.

We can also influence people with their senses. For example, a study found that if you put a lemon cleaning scent in the room where people are eating cookies, they are more likely to clean up after themselves. There are a lot of ways to influence people's behaviors so they think they're doing things out of their own volition, but they're really being unconsciously manipulated by stimuli in their environment. Unconscious neurological processes play a big role in influence.

"We're being influenced all the time by everything in our environment."

As we understand the brain better and you say things to me like, "I can know your behavior ten seconds before you do it by studying the brain," how do you think about that power as it permeates more of society?

It helps if you can accept that you *are* your brain. I see patients with brain lesions that can completely change their personalities. Our sense of self is really just a narrative that's created in the brain that we can then disrupt and change. I mean, now we're using neural implants to treat intractable movement disorders and psychiatric illnesses. But ultimately that's going to move into cognitive enhancement, where we can actually just go in with electrodes and manipulate people's emotions—and maybe someday their memory capacity or attention spans. But that opens up the possibility that people can potentially get hacked, right? Other people could potentially control your electrodes and directly manipulate your thoughts and behavior.

It's also a myth that we only use 10 percent of our brains. We use all of it all the time, but we're only consciously aware of a very little bit of what's happening in our brains. If we could let go of our need to be so much in control we'd be more at peace with ourselves. We have to learn to say, "Yeah, my brain's making decisions unconsciously. It's being affected by what's in its environment. I'm not necessarily making rational decisions based on the intrinsic value of things. And that's okay." Perhaps our unconscious has free will and we're just the last to know about it.

We're being influenced all the time by everything in our environment. Certain very strong people, with strong personalities or ideas can easily slip in and have a strong influence over many people if their voices are loud enough, if they have enough to say, or if they do something that grabs a sufficient amount of attention. It doesn't take that much to influence people.

Leonard Mlodinow opened my eyes to how much of what happens is on a subconscious level and how that's manipulated against us by advertisers. Looking five or ten years down the road, where do you see this trend going? Advertising is already so powerful.

Len's a friend and colleague, and he even consulted with me when he was writing *Subliminal*. Advertisers are getting more and more insidious. They are openly admitting that they're using techniques that we understand about psychology to make products more likely to be addictive. For instance, with games or apps, if you introduce a reinforcement schedule that's not consistent, that's random, you're more likely to become addicted because you never know when the next reward is going to come.

If there's a question of how we gain more control over ourselves, I think part of it is spending time detaching. Be outdoors, go for a walk, find time away from all the stimulation. Remove yourself from all the incoming stimuli that's influencing you, and force yourself to just detach. It's hard for people to do, but nature has a really positive effect on the psyche. You're filling your brain with positive, or at least neutral, stimuli.

I want to ask for your advice. Let's assume I'm a young person just starting out in my career. I don't necessarily want to be famous, but I want to be influential. I want my messages to be shared. What advice would you have from your purview of neuroscience, impulse, and subconscious behavior?

Be the best you that you can be. I'm going to paraphrase advice from two people who I can't believe I'm quoting in the same breath: Jay-Z and Steve Martin. Jay-Z once said that everybody has something in them, a talent, and our job is to find out what it is and then nurture it. And Steve Martin would tell comedians asking for advice on how to get famous, "Just be good. Just be good consistently and over time. There's no shortcut."

So find that talent in yourself, whether it's the ability to play an instrument or communicate or play a sport or write books. Practice it and develop it. And put yourself out there. It's hard for people who are more introverted, but you have to be able to sell it or connect with people who can.

For me, I was just doing what I love to do, and a scout from Discovery Channel contacted me out of the blue after they saw an online talk I had given. They then flew me to London to audition to host a new series. Because they found me pretty last minute, I didn't have the pressure of the whole long audition process that some other people were faced with. It enabled me to be pretty relaxed and calm and, I guess, relatable when I did the audition.

I got the job and went on the road just a few weeks later to shoot the show! They flew me around the world to meet people with extraordinary abilities who could do mind-blowing things. I was tasked with trying to figure out scientifically how they could do these seemingly impossible feats. It was a whirlwind and I just learned on the job, and then things snowballed from there.

I was very fortunate to have been given this opportunity, but it only happened because I was doing the thing I enjoyed doing and making sure it got out there, and eventually someone noticed.

Who has been influential in your life and career?

I was lucky enough to have some very strong women role models, like my grandmother, when I was coming up in the male-dominated world of science. My grandmother was one of the first female contractors in New York in the 1960s. She supervised all these very rugged male construction workers on site. In her time this was just unheard of.

And then there was Professor Susan Iverson, one of my PhD supervisors at Oxford. Not only was she head of the Department of Experimental Psychology, she was also a pro-vice chancellor of the university. She's a strong, intelligent woman who was also kind and generous with her time—a really great role model.

But outside of my personal life, in pop culture, there wasn't really anyone influencing me in terms of what I could be as a scientist. I used to think you had to be nerdy. You couldn't be cool or attractive in any way. You couldn't be feminine.

You had to be like Bill Nye the Science Guy?

You had to be Bill Nye, exactly. Funnily enough, I ended up meeting him at a conference at Google when I was an adult, and he became a real friend and mentor as I began my journey into science communication. But there were no female Bill Nyes when I was coming up. I would love it if young girls today could see women like me and others excelling in our fields as scientists and think, "Hey, I can do that too." I want to lead by example and show young girls that they can be women as well as scientists. We don't have to fit into any stereotypes.

If you want to be influential, or if you are already influential, pay it forward. Give advice. Mentor people. Put your ego aside. See what you can learn from other people as well, because you don't know everything. If you're constantly open and evolving, you're going to influence others in the best way possible. Be humble, and be true to yourself.

I'm going to give you a billboard, and millions of people are going to see it every day. You get to share an important message with the world related to influence and your work and research. What do you want it to say?

I would say something like, "Be true to yourself, and the rest will follow," or "Find the thing you're good at and enjoy doing, and keep doing it."

EDITOR'S NOTES

Berlin's point that everyone is unconsciously influenced by the world around them recalls Dan Ariely and Moran Cerf, who maintain that engineering people's choices or environments is more effective than direct motivation.

"Find the thing you're good at and enjoy doing, and keep doing it."

—Heather Berlin

"None of us operates in the same way throughout the course of even a single day."

Moran Cerf is a professor of neuroscience and business at the Kellogg School of Management and the Alfred P. Sloan Professor at the American Film Institute, where he teaches science in film and is a consultant to Hollywood productions. He holds multiple patents. Cerf's work has been published in academic journals such as *Nature* and has appeared in *Wired*, *Scientific American*, BBC, CNN, *The Atlantic*, *Time*, *Forbes*, and more.

Cerf's research uses neuroscience to understand the underlying mechanisms of our psychology, emotion, decision-making, and dreams. He has made much of his research accessible to the general public via talks at TED, TEDx, PopTech, and The World Economic Forum.

Prior to his academic career, Cerf worked as a hacker in the cybersecurity industry. He is the cofounder of ThinkAlike and B-Cube. Importantly, he is right-handed.

The Architecture of Influence

Moran Cerf

Ok, so you are a French-Israeli neuroscientist, a professor of business, and a former hacker. How do you define influence?

Influence, from a neurological perspective, is the ability to change someone else's behavior. The question is, on what scale can you effect behavioral change, and how much effort does it take? If I can do something that changes your behavior, I have influence, but it is low influence. If I can do the same thing but affect a million people, I have high influence. The most influential person is the one who can can affect many people with very little effort.

Understanding what humans actually respond to can reduce how much effort you need to put into influencing others, yet those responses are not always intuitive. For instance, we tend to think that providing more information will change behavior, but it does not. If you ask people what they need to do to lose weight, they will give the right answer: eat healthier and exercise more. So why are not they doing those things? They have all the information they need. It just does not lead to a behavior change.

Knowledge does not change behavior. The two things that do are empathy and choice architecture. Politicians get it. You might have noticed that they do not really compete to educate you. They use fear, engagement, and curiosity, because at the end of the day they know the information they give you does not matter. It is how they speak, what emotions they trigger. That is a clever use of empathy, and it is what gives them influence.

I will come back to empathy, but first let me unpack the other big component of changing behavior: designing the architecture of choice. It means you structure the world such that people have almost no choice but to behave the way you want.

Let us say we want more people to sign up to be organ donors. If we tell them how important it is, it will not change their behavior at all. But if we add a line to the DMV form that says, "Check this box to NOT donate your organs," we will get a lot more organ donors. Why? People have a tendency to not want to change things, or to not make decisions, and adding an opt-out box adds a decision. People are essentially too lazy to check the box. Multiple countries in Europe have done this successfully: understanding people's psychology enabled them to change population-level behavior. They architected the way people will behave.

There are tons of studies on banking in Africa, where low-income people in particular were just terrible at saving money and nothing seemed to be working to shift that behavior. But then banks instituted a fundamental change: they made it very easy to deposit funds but very, very hard to withdraw them. Now, to put money in your account you simply send a text. To get money out, you text, get a token back, then have to go to a specific place and put the token in, and so on—and now people save more. Telling an entire population to save more did not work. Educating them about the importance of pensions did not work. Choice architecture worked.

How do you design good choice architecture? What makes it so effective?

People are not good at making complex decisions. They prefer to make simple ones. People tend to get tired when making too many choices, so understanding that is key to creating choice architecture. Generally, knowing people's brain flaws is what you need to create a good architecture. For instance, people sometimes make decisions differently in the morning versus the evening. That is why some banks will only call you during specific times when they know you are more likely to make

"Good influencers have this ability to see the world from someone else's viewpoint and then create things that are engaging for that person."

riskier decisions. Knowing when to use humor is a big one, too, and when to really pamper people with attention.

One major component to building a good choice architecture for efficient influence is empathy. I have to be able to put myself in your shoes to understand what might influence you. Good influencers have this ability to see the world from someone else's viewpoint and then create things that are engaging for that person.

If I am talking to a tech person who really likes data, I might use short sentences containing specific facts. If I needed to influence that person I would rely on research. I would put myself in a mode—data-driven—that would resonate with them. I would adapt my behavior based on what I understand about them to change theirs. If I had to deliver the same information to my four-year-old nephew as I did to the tech person, I would not talk the same way. I would choose a totally different way of communicating the information. And that is what I call empathy. To be influential, you have to be able to understand how best to get information to as many brains as possible: figure out how each brain works, and communicate the same ideas to each one differently.

The thing is, empathy is generally hard to teach. Some people just have it, and some people do not have it. But it can be quantified. You can write down what you think a person is going through. If nine times out of ten times you perfectly hit the experience of the other person, well, you are really good at empathy.

If you are someone who is not good at empathy and wants to get better, one thing that seems to work is asking questions and being in the same room physically. Research shows that if you ask loads of questions, like that is your sole aim rather than eliciting specific answers, it gives you information that you did not know would be relevant. You will get what topics make the person laugh and what makes them embarrassed or uncomfortable. So if you are trying to learn to be more empathetic, sit down with someone and just ask questions for twenty minutes.

It is actually quite important to do this in person. There are a lot of communication cues that do not carry over into other venues like video calls. Facial expressions are only the beginning. For instance, if the temperature is very cold, some aspects of what you are going to say will be influenced by that; it is important to both be in the same space experiencing the same atmosphere while we communicate. If we both have a nice view in front of us, we are going to talk slower than if we do not. If it is evening versus morning, we are going to talk differently.

Beyond that, more and more studies show that we actually communicate not just with language and gestures but also with the odors we emit. It turns out that smells are crucial to communication—this is especially true for communicating negative emotions. If you start crying, it will change the dynamics of the conversation because it will make me realize that you are experiencing some kind of pain. If we are in the same room, I will inhale a molecule produced by your tears that will decrease my testosterone by 80 percent. I will become less aggressive. This means that having the same argument in person instead of online changes the participants' experience.

If you are in the same room with someone, you have a little bit stronger ability to influence them. Like, Justin Bieber cannot be in the same room with his fans to communicate to them, but the fans themselves can be with each other. And when fan clubs get together, it is been shown to increase the influence of whoever they are a fan of. So there is something to the physicality of not just me and you, but also you and others.

You have developed influence in your career. Are these the tactics that you use? What do you feel has made you a leader in your research field?

There is a saying among scientists that we all make the same mistakes at the end of the day. I wish I were better at applying the things that I preach, but I do try. First of all, I carefully curate the people I spend time with. Our research shows that you are influenced greatly by the people around you. Not just by the content of your conversations or by what they might do, but literally just by being around them.

Say you are someone who is always running late, and you want to develop the habit of being on time. If you surround yourself with punctual people, you will get better at being on time without expending conscious effort to improve. You will just see that they always leave a little bit earlier. You will see that they start talking about where they need to be beforehand. This is catching.

Or take being funny, which is very important to me. As a scientist, no one trains you to do presentations. You are trained to do research. I decided humor was a skill I wanted to learn, and who better to learn from than comedians? They are great at going on stage and keeping people engaged the entire time. So instead of hiring a speaking coach, I decided to hang out with comedians. I wanted their skill to rub off on me. I met one comedian I really liked, Whitney Cummings, and told her, "It is you. I am choosing you as my guide." As it turned out, she liked the brain science I brought to the table. I shadowed her and went to her shows, and she came to me to learn about the brain. We had this perfect kind of match.

When I spend time with Whitney and my other comedian friends, I am not trying to get funnier by replicating their jokes. The act of spending time with them helps me learn how they think about the world, and how comedic timing works, and their way of reversing a sentence to make it funny.

You cannot prioritize everything, though, so if you identify something as particularly important you may need to give up something else. For instance, what I give up is making small choices. If I go to a restaurant with friends or go see a movie, I never choose where we go. My focus is on curating the best company that I can. That is the choice I have made. Now that I am with them, I give up the small choices; by doing that, I am giving these people influence over me. I am saying, "You control my life in this domain."

Do you have any tips, tricks, or tactics to pursue becoming more influential by leveraging current neuroscience?

It is useful to know yourself—not only your personality, but your brain, which has a dynamic profile. None of us operates in the same way throughout the course of even a single day. You might make decisions better in the morning while I make them better in the evening. You might make decisions better in a room by yourself, and I, when I am surrounded by ten people advising me.

There is no right or wrong here. The faster you learn what your brain profile is, the faster you can determine when you can be most influential and when you can be most open to the influence of others. This is information you can put to practical use. By knowing that you are most open to new ideas in the morning, for instance, you might schedule certain meetings for that time.

Have an objective neuroscientist look at your brain and give you some readings. It does not take that much time, and it gives you a different data point on who you are that could be important. The results might not align with who you think you are. Once you know who you truly are, though, you might be able to change your behavior to better suit the reality of your brain profile.

For instance, the neuroscientist could have you play a game and determine that you are extremely risk-averse when you thought you were, in fact, very risk-tolerant. If you were to lose money, you

"Our research shows that you are influenced greatly by the people around you. Not just by the content of your conversations or by what they might do, but literally just by being around them."

would be devastated. This knowledge could lead you to manage your affairs very differently.

I am a young person who wants to become a leader and become more influential. What would you tell me to do?

My advice to anyone who wants to be more influential is to make many friends and figure out who they are to you. Who is your funny friend? Your dependable friend? Your friend who always has new ideas? Diversity here is really, really useful.

And study your brain. Start by keeping a diary to monitor your behavior, which enables you to observe changes. This does not have to be exhaustive. For one week, whenever you have made a decision, write down what your options were and what the conditions were. For example, say you were offered a few choices at a restaurant. You put in your notebook, "I went to a restaurant at noon, and I had to choose salmon, steak, or salad. I was very stressed, I was very hungry (and so on). I chose salmon."

And then a day or so afterward, write down how happy you were with the choice you made.

Just by doing that you will start noticing things. You will get to know yourself better. Maybe you are on the whole much happier with your choices than you thought. Or a particular type of decision actually does not matter to you. Like, you put a lot of thought into the steak, salmon, and salad, but in the end you do not even remember if you were happy with your meal or not. It turns out that decision did not really matter.

This exercise will teach you a lot, not just about your personality but about what is important or not, and maybe what things lead to good choices. You might come away saying, "You know what, I am happier with the choices I make in the evening than in the morning. I make better choices when I am with this friend than with that one."

Next, imagine the people you want to influence. Say you are a musician. Imagine what your audience would look like and what they would do, and see at what moments of your day you are more or less like them. Use the moments that you are most like them to connect and build influence. For instance, send out a tweet with the language that you think will appeal to them. Once you realize who you are and who you want to interact with, empathy becomes easier.

You have a billboard the world can see. What does it say?

Do not believe everything you think.

That is the tagline of everything. In the past, we were taught that we could always trust ourselves, no matter what else was going on in the world. But the last few years have brought terms like "fake news" and "alternative facts" to the fore. They indicate that people are going to try to be influencing you, but you have your mental faculties and skepticism that allow you to vet information and to sort out what is right from what is not.

We are heading to a stage that is even worse. We will be attacking internal truths. Right now let us say you and I are talking to each other. If later on someone asks you what you did during this time, you would say, "I spoke to Moran." There is almost nothing that would make you change your mind about that, because you have your memory of this time, and you count on your memory more than anything else.

There are about forty thousand people in the world right now who have cheap implants inside their brains for clinical purposes. You can actually hack into those things. And when you do that, you are not just hacking into it—you are making a person change their mind internally. Can you imagine a world where someone could hack into your brain and change your mind and you would have no idea that it happened? That is where we are going.

People never doubt their own minds. We say, "Well, if I think it, it must have happened." We believe that because we have experienced it, it must be true. That is what is changing right now. We started to worry about fake news when it was too late; it had already affected our systems. Fake internal truth is something that has not happened yet. But scientists are playing with it, and I would like people to know about it right now.

The only way to prevent being fundamentally influenced like this, without your knowledge or consent, is to practice skepticism—even of your own beliefs.

EDITOR'S NOTES

Cerf mentions the nonverbal signals we lose when we don't communicate in person. Zandan expands on the importance of those subtle and often unconscious signals—and how important they are for influence.

"Do not believe everything you think."

—Moran Cerf

"I've been able to prove that we've evolved four very broad styles of thinking and behaving that align with our dopamine, serotonin, testosterone, and estrogen systems in the brain."

Helen Fisher, PhD, is a biological anthropologist who has conducted extensive research and written six books on the evolution and future of human sex, love, and marriage; gender differences in the brain; and how your personality style shapes who you are and who you love. She is the cofounder of a consulting company, NeuroColor, that has used her understanding of brain science to develop a revolutionary new personality tool to create better outcomes for individuals, teams, and organizations.

Helen is a senior research fellow at the Kinsey Institute and chief scientific advisor to Match.com. She is currently using her knowledge of brain chemistry to discuss the neuroscience of business leadership and innovation. For her work in communicating anthropology to the lay public, Helen has received the American Anthropological Association's Anthropology in Media and Distinguished Service awards.

Brains, Biology, and Behavior

Helen Fisher

Let's start with the relationship between sexuality, influence, and power. How does sexuality influence our relationships?

Sexuality is an ancient drive emanating from one of the most primitive parts of the brain. It plays a role in a lot of relationships. I don't think sex plays a role in all relationships. I mean, I think that one can read the newspaper and respond to the influence of political leaders or poets or musicians without including sexuality.

We've evolved three distinctly different brain systems that play a role in our mating behavior:

1. The sex drive
2. Feelings of intense romantic love
3. Feelings of deep attachment and commitment to a partner

We're very strongly programmed to respond to all three of these basic brain systems.

I do not think, as a lot of feminists do, that the sex act is about power. It does certainly play a role in influence, however. If you're dying to have sex with somebody, then what they say to you on the telephone, or by text or email, is going to influence how you act. You're going to dress in a certain way to look sexy. You're going to try to listen. You're going to try to say the right thing. You're going to try to coax them into the bedroom. You're going to try to please.

When I say that sex is not all about power, what I mean is that in a good sexual relationship, both partners are trying to please. Both are trying to influence. Both are trying to be seductive and feel seductive and court and mate. It's a duet. It's a mating dance. It's not a power game, exactly.

As you think about the split of those three different brain systems, which of them affects our behavior the most?

I'd say the weakest of the three is actually the sex drive. I mean, if you ask somebody to go to bed with you and they say, "No, thank you," you probably don't kill yourself. Whereas around the world, people do kill themselves when they can't get romantic love. They live for love. They kill for love. They die for love.

The fact that the brain is wired this way is exceedingly important. In fact, the part of the brain that pumps out dopamine—which gives you that feeling of romantic love—lies right near the base of the brain, near brain regions that orchestrate thirst and hunger.

Thirst and hunger keep you alive today. Romantic love drives you to fall in love and form a pair and send your DNA into tomorrow. Romantic love is a survival mechanism, a drive. We care very much about it.

Attachment is important too, though. When you discover your partner has cheated on you or is abandoning you, those broken feelings of deep attachment can drive people to murder or suicide. They can become very jealous. They can try to seduce in unusual ways. They can begin to stalk.

This is why I say the sex drive is the weakest of the three. Someone will get frustrated if you don't want to have sex with them. They'll be disappointed. Maybe they'll sulk or get mad. But they don't kill themselves, and they don't tend to kill you. The much stronger influencers are the brain systems for romantic love and attachment.

How conscious are we of all this? If I know about it, can I control it?

Some of it is conscious, and some of it is subterranean, or unconscious, or preconscious. I mean, for example, suddenly you have a very strong reaction when you smell a chocolate chip cookie. If you ask somebody why they responded to that, they might tell you that they love chocolate chip cookies and that they grew up with chocolate chip cookies. Or that every time they went to a certain grandmother's house, she made chocolate chip cookies and, while they loved the cookies, they were also very happy there for other reasons. But they won't tell you the "ultimate" reason that they like these treats: because millions of years ago humanity evolved a sweet tooth for adaptive reasons.

In short: almost all behaviors have a "proximate" cause—what you *think* the cause of your behavior is. But there's also the ultimate cause, which we often know nothing about. For example, you can say, "I'm in love with her," or "I feel deeply committed to her," or "I'd really like to get her in bed. She's hot." Those are your conscious, proximate reasons for doing something. Underneath that, there are ancient drives that evolved to make us act in certain ways—your human inheritance, your human nature. A good 50 percent of who we are comes out of our genetics and biology. Most people aren't aware of that.

Here's an example. Some people are very traditional while other people are very risk-taking. The traditional people will say to you, "I grew up in a traditional household. I like those values." Well, they won't tell you that there's also a gene in the serotonin system associated with social norm conformity—a gene that they inherited.

How much are people who are influential tapping into these systems as tools of influence? Does this stuff just kind of happen naturally, and you have it or you don't?

We are attracted to power. We are attracted to influential people for good Darwinian reasons. They can provide some of the things we want in life.

Under this broader definition of influence as related to sexuality, who do you consider to be really influential?

Almost anybody can be. Take a poor neighborhood, underprivileged, not exactly the sort of place where we think people of serious influence operate. But say there's this handsome young man who's very good at playing basketball. Everybody thinks he's very cool, so he's got power. He's got sexual power. More women will be attracted to him just because he's handsome and charismatic and well-coordinated, and perhaps he's also kind. That's one kind of influence.

Then there's someone like Barack Obama, a man of real integrity, a man of influence. I would guess that there are an awful lot of women who would go to bed with him if they had the opportunity. Or how about a rock star? I mean, all they're good at is creating a tune and playing it on an instrument. But they've got money and stature—influence. Lots of groupies are willing to have sex with them just to be near that power and influence.

I'm an anthropologist. Even in hunting and gathering societies, there are some individuals who are called "big men." They have more wives. Why do they have more wives? Because they're big men. They are influential. They have social power.

Eighty-six percent of world cultures permit polygamy (many wives). Men with power and influence are able to have multiple wives simultaneously, a harem. It's pretty standard that "big men" in one field or another are going to have sexual influence and romantic influence and reproductive influence for solid Darwinian reasons. For millions of years, women needed to find a partner who could help them raise their young. As a result, women are attracted to men of influence because they will acquire his resources and be better able to raise healthy babies. This is absolute standard Darwinian mating psychology: people of influence tend to get more mating opportunities.

Does it work in the opposite direction as well, where there's a "big woman" who has influence and is able to attract more men, or is it asymmetric?

Anthropologists have long thought that it was asymmetric and that men were really threatened by a woman with a great deal of power. I think that is a holdover from our farming days. In hunting and gathering societies, a woman who was a very good gatherer, a very good singer, a very good talker, a very good healer would most likely have more partners than a woman who limped, was missing teeth, had poor eyesight, and was bad at her basic duties.

But I do think we're going to see more and more that women in a position of power are going to attract more men. Men like money just the way women do. If a woman has a lot of money and she's good looking, men are going to flock to her. We're talking about basic survival here. People want to be around successful people. People want to be around happy people. People want to be around people with money, land, education, or other forms of influence and power.

Let's talk about the MeToo movement. Is our awareness evolving? As we become more conscious of it and hear the stories of it, are people more aware of how influenced they are by it?

Yes, absolutely. I'm doing a study with Match.com right now. We asked more than five thousand single men and women a lot of questions about the #MeToo movement. Some 40 percent of single men in America today are more reserved around female colleagues at work, and 33 percent of men are more reserved with a woman while on a date. Moreover, 35 percent of men are more reserved around women in public and 28 percent are more careful with what they post on social media. The MeToo movement is definitely affecting men (and women). Women are gaining power and influence.

You study sexuality as it relates to human dynamics. How do you think about that for yourself?

I know a great deal about sex and love and marriage. I've written several books on these topics. They sell around the world, and I give a lot of speeches on all this. But when it comes to my personal life, I'm pretty much like everyone else. I mean, you can know every single ingredient in a piece of chocolate cake and then sit down and eat the cake and enjoy it every bit as much as anyone else.

I've done a lot of stupid things when I was in love, just like everybody else. When you're madly in love with somebody, it's very difficult to control those feelings. But I'm probably better at it than a lot of people, only because I've learned what makes relationships successful. For example, if a man doesn't want me, I don't keep pursuing him. I've learned a lot from all my years of studying love. But I'm not really different from anybody else. These are basic motivation systems, sex drive, feelings of intense romantic love, and feelings of deep attachment. We all have them to one degree or another. We all try to use them to influence or modify our

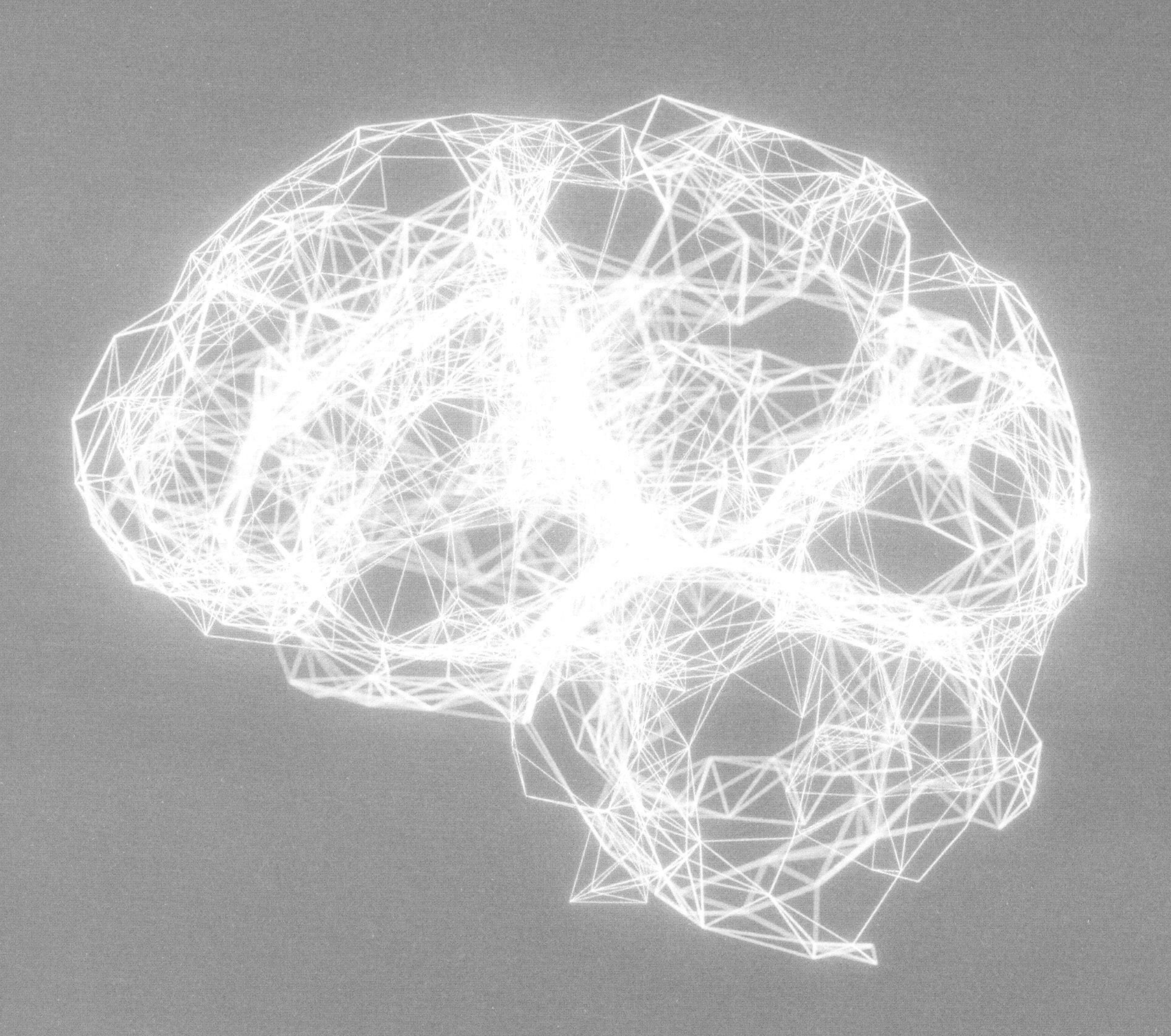

behavior—or the behavior of others—sometimes when it's appropriate, sometimes not.

Let's say I want to be more influential, maybe not with a direct intention to use sexuality to achieve that, but to be more influential in my career and to create positive change. What advice would you give me based on your research and understanding?

Well, I'd suggest you learn more about human nature—and then I'd invite you to behave in ways to *naturally* connect with and influence others. But to explain: I study the biology of personality—some 50 percent of who you are. And I've been able to prove that we've evolved four very broad styles of thinking and behaving that align with our dopamine, serotonin, testosterone, and estrogen systems in the brain. So I would get to know who someone really is on these four biological scales and then treat them the way they want to be treated. I'll just briefly go through those.

If someone's very expressive of the traits in the dopamine system, I call them an Explorer. They tend to be novelty-seeking, risk-taking, curious, creative, spontaneous, energetic, and mentally flexible.

If someone tends to be very expressive of the traits in the serotonin system, I call them a Builder. Builders tend to be traditional, conventional. They follow the rules. They respect authority. They tend to be concrete rather than theoretical thinkers. They like rules and schedules and plans. And they tend to be more traditionally religious.

The third broad style of thinking and behaving is linked with the testosterone system. I call these people Directors. They tend to be analytical, logical, direct, decisive, tough-minded, skeptical, fair, and good at things like math, engineering, computers, or music. They are often very spatial.

The fourth is high estrogen. I call people in this category Negotiators. They're contextual, holistic, synthetic, long-term thinkers. They deal well with ambiguity. They're imaginative. They tend to have good people skills and verbal skills. They're good at reading posture, gesture, and tone of voice. They tend to be nurturing, trusting, and emotionally expressive as well.

So if I were to give anybody any advice for dealing with others, I would recommend that they understand not only who they are (on these four biologically based personality scales), but also who the other person is. And then I would discuss matters in ways that they can hear me. I no longer believe in the Golden Rule: Do unto others as you would have them do unto you. Instead, I believe in the Platinum Rule: Do unto others as they would have done unto themselves—and you will reach into their brain and influence them.

For a few examples: if I'm talking to somebody who's very high on the dopamine scale, an Explorer,

I'll give them the big theory first. I try to give them novelty, excitement, and ideas. And I express my own energy and ideas.

If I'm dealing with a person who is very high on the serotonin scale, a Builder, I don't give the big theory first. I give all the details instead. I try to be very calm. I try to be a little bit more formal. I'll play down the risky ideas and go for more traditional values and concepts.

If I'm with somebody who is very high testosterone, a Director, I'll get straight to the point. If I'm with somebody who's very high estrogen, a Negotiator, I might start out by talking about family or feelings—engaging them with a more personal tone.

The more you can understand the brain, the more you can begin to understand biologically who someone is and then present your data and ideas *in a way that enables that person to hear them.* As I said recently in the *Harvard Business Review*, "If you can understand the brain, you can understand anybody." So if you want to learn a lot more on this topic, you can get it on the internet, on my website www.TheAnatomyOfLove, or in my book *Why Him? Why Her?*

Is there a style that's more influential? You've said world leaders tend to be serotonin people.

World leaders can be highly influential in different ways. Obama, for example, is probably high estrogen. Abraham Lincoln was probably

"The Platinum Rule: Do unto others as they would have done unto themselves."

very high estrogen, too. High-estrogen people are likely to work contextually and long-term, as well as to genuinely fight for the under-privileged, make decisions slowly and be cooperative and consensus-building.

Then there's somebody like Putin: high testosterone. He's direct, tough-minded, and aggressive. That's probably why Putin and Obama didn't understand each other but Trump, Putin, Xi Jinping, and Kim Jong-un all do. They're all high testosterone. And they are all likely to regard Obama as weak. Obama isn't weak. He's just more of a Negotiator—more of a long-term, consensus-building thinker, the high-estrogen style of behaving. Then take Mike Pence, a fellow who expresses a lot of the traits of the serotonin system. He's traditional, religious, and cautious, a very different kind of leader than either Obama or Trump.

We're all a combination of all of these four brain systems, of course. For example, I express a lot of the traits of the dopamine and the estrogen systems and very few traits of the testosterone and serotonin systems. But no two people are exactly alike. I'm an identical twin, and even my twin sister and I are not exactly alike. Each of us has a unique personality. But there are patterns to nature, patterns to culture, and patterns to personality.

I started a new company, actually, called NeuroColor. With my colleagues there, I have constructed a second-generation questionnaire, based on all of my data from the first (which has now been taken by fourteen million people in forty countries). My colleagues at NeuroColor now go into companies and help individuals understand themselves, and perhaps more importantly, show them how to interact far more effectively with their colleagues and clients.

Psychologists have told us that all of our behavior is learned in our childhood. It's simply not true. A good 40 to 60 percent of who you are comes out of your biology. People have biologically based personalities. And when you understand these intricacies and variations of human nature, you can win.

It's interesting to think about leading a company. Some of the traits that seem to make a good leader aren't the traits you need to run a company long-term; wouldn't you need the serotonin people to support you?

That's very well said. In our company, the cofounder is very high testosterone and dopamine. And as mentioned, I'm very high estrogen and dopamine. We don't have any serotonin in our leadership. So we have had to hire people who are more expressive of the traits in the serotonin system. They're our accountants. They send out the materials. They keep the daily details in order. That's the beauty of this. It's not just knowing who you are but how to build a team and how to get people to innovate *together.*

For example, people of these four different styles of thinking and behaving are going to innovate differently. The high dopamine folks are going to innovate with new ideas. They'll invent the newest mousetrap. The high-testosterone type is going to make it work technically. The high-serotonin type is going to create the process by which they can build and produce it. And those most expressive of the traits in the estrogen system are going to hire all the PR people, deal with the press, advertise the product, and sell it.

I've got one last question for you. I'm going to give you a billboard that millions of people will drive by every day. I'd like you to share some counsel, something about influence, with them. What do you want it to say?

If you want to connect with somebody, understand their brain.

EDITOR'S NOTES

Fisher tells us that we have to understand how someone's brain works in order to reach them, which is the key to Carmen Simon's discussion of crafting individualized rewards.

"If you want to connect with somebody, understand their brain."

—Helen Fisher

"I think about where we could reduce the gap between how we should be performing and how we actually are performing."

Despite our intentions, why do we so often fail to act in our own best interest? Why do we overvalue things that we've worked to put together? What are the forces that influence our behavior? **Dan Ariely**, James B. Duke Professor of Psychology & Behavioral Economics at Duke University, is dedicated to answering these questions and others in order to help people live more sensible—if not rational—lives.

Dan is a founding member of the Center for Advanced Hindsight, co-creator of the film documentary *(Dis)Honesty: The Truth About Lies*, and a three-time *New York Times* bestselling author. His books include *Predictably Irrational*, *The Upside of Irrationality*, *The Honest Truth About Dishonesty*, *Irrationally Yours*, *Payoff*, *Dollars and Sense*, and *Amazing Decisions*.

In 2013 Bloomberg recognized Dan as one of their Top 50 Most Influential thinkers. He has a bi-weekly advice column in *The Wall Street Journal* called "Ask Ariely." Dan can be found at www.danariely.com.

Less Friction, More Motivation

Dan Ariely

We'll start at the very top. How would you describe what you study?

So the official title is behavioral economics, but the real thing I'm studying is how to get people to act slightly differently. I want to know how to get people a little bit closer to achieving our human potential. We underperform in so many ways, and it saddens me. We misspend our time, money, and health, and we're destroying the global environment. I think about where we could reduce the gap between how we should be performing and how we actually are performing.

You're setting out to "improve the human performance gap" with research. How do you go about changing people's behaviors?

The big lesson from behavioral economics is that the environment matters: if we can control the environment, we can change the behavior. Some things are harder to change than others. If we have access to people's calendars, for instance, we can control their time. It's not trivial, but we can do it. By contrast, it's very difficult to control people's physical money—you can't access that complete environment. On the other hand, when they have electronic wallets, that gives us better access and enables us to have a little more control over that environment. Can we control people's health? Well, if we have electronic medical records, we could do a little bit better job of that, yes.

The behaviors we're most likely to improve are one-off decisions that stay with us a long time, like signing up for a 401(k). You have to do it once when you get to a new job, which is when you'll set up your defaults. If I can help you make the decision in a better way just that one time, that decision will stay with you. It will serve you.

Or take a big issue like energy saving. It's easier for me to change your decision about what refrigerator to buy, therefore reducing your energy footprint, than to get you to turn heating or air conditioning on and off all the time. Or, as another example, it's easier for me to get you to install a smart thermostat than to get you to manually set an old-fashioned thermostat every day to save energy.

So I start with figuring out what the ideal path is for behavior. Then I look at what things are holding people back from achieving that behavior and how I can move those obstacles out of the way.

Sounds like you're resetting the behaviors we have on autopilot in order to make the world run better.

If you can put the behaviors that we know are the right ones on autopilot, then yes. It's just very, very hard to make the right decision every time. Having things set in the right way from the get-go helps.

My favorite metaphor for behavioral change is sending rockets to space. When you send a rocket to space, there are two general tasks: dealing with friction and dealing with fuel. You're trying to give the rocket the smallest amount of friction along with the largest amount of fuel.

In the world of behavioral change, friction is how far the natural behavior is from the ideal behavior (the farther away, the greater the friction), and the fuel represents motivation. Friction is usually the easier of the two to deal with because it's determined by the constraints of the system. You can see it, and you can measure it. You can understand all the elements and all the possibilities. But motivation is a bit more complex.

Let's say I look at what gets people to eat healthily. The friction would be how difficult it is to find the healthy food, how much money and time it costs to prepare, and so on. Because the analysis of friction starts with the current system, it is easier to see what to change within the system to help people make better choices. But increasing motivation is harder to figure out. I could try to motivate you to make better food choices by telling you that your kids would like you more or by giving you points for eating healthily. There are so many options, but it's almost impossible for us to know in advance which one will resonate with you. Motivation by itself is a harder path.

“Influence is a system that first deals with the friction and then adds motivational elements to encourage the desired activity.”

Political campaign strategists often use a similar analogy. Most of the attention in political campaigns goes toward the fuel—convincing people to vote for your candidate. When in reality, 50 percent of political success is based on actually getting somebody who already supports you to the voting booth. We overstress who you vote for while not really addressing the friction of getting to the voting booth.

That's right. For that political example, I would say that a world without friction is a world in which people wake up in the voting booth. Now, some people would wake up in the voting booth and leave without voting. Those are the people who really don't want to vote.

But the people who would vote if they woke up there but wouldn't vote otherwise, those are the people who are not voting because of friction. But, you know, it's pretty hard to get people to wake up in a voting booth, so now we have to think about motivation and how increased motivation might overcome the friction.

One example of such motivation is the peer angle. Saying "Well, everybody else is voting" gets more people to vote. We've also looked at getting kids to motivate their parents to vote. In some countries, like in the United States, you get this little sticker that says, "I voted," to make people feel better about it, and that has a social effect. There are all kinds of other things that we could do to add to the motivation equation.

In my view, influence is a system that first deals with the friction and then adds motivational elements to encourage the desired activity. It all starts by figuring out what people do naturally and then how we can get them to be closer to what we think of as ideal.

Would influential people be those who are conscious of and can move others into that system?

When we think about behavioral change from this perspective, there are actually two types of influential people. One is the type of person who could actually build those systems. The other is someone who provides some motivation for action.

Let's look at the first type. I would say I fall into this category, where being influential is not about charisma or reputation but about creating systems that enable ongoing behavioral change. For example, I've been involved in designing a new food labeling system in Israel that encourages healthier choices. Healthy food gets a green circle, and unhealthy food gets a red circle; it sounds very simple, but we found that this system has a big effect on behavior. By getting the government of Israel to adopt this, I would say I've been an influential person because I created a system that is going to influence behavior.

The second type of influential person is someone who can provide additional motivation. So if I say something like, "I voted. You should vote as well," and then that person decides to vote because I did, this makes me an influential person of the second type. And if I can make this happen on a large scale, now I am really influential.

Take financial decision-making. There are plenty of people who write books and give lectures about how to manage our finances in a better way. And I'm not against that approach. But if you're really going to get people to change their behavior around money, banks need to create a different process where people understand the consequences of their actions and where they have better financial tools, more automated savings, and so on.

The biggest system changes can happen through the government, which is why I focus much of my own work on them. Governments are sources of terrible things, but they also have a huge scale. If you get somebody from a government to do something in a better way, like label food in a better way or create a new rule to open college savings accounts for kids, or whatever, you'll see massive improvements in behaviors.

Society celebrates the people who are able to motivate more than the people who invent great systems. Most people seem to think of influential people as bucket number two and not as bucket number one.

Yes, but bucket number one is incredibly important. The people who designed Google Calendar, or whatever calendar you use, have had a huge influence on your life, for good and bad.

A calendar basically helps people set up more appointments with greater ease, which is a terrible thing to do. You see empty time on your calendar and you say, "Let's make another appointment." So the people who designed calendars this way have cost those who use those calendars lots of meetings and lots of wasted time. Or take social media, which was designed with the intention to get people to spend more time being exposed to ads rather than being productive. The people who designed those systems have been very influential, though I think not in a net positive way.

It's not that type two influencers aren't important; the scale and type of their impact is just different. How much did Al Gore move the needle on the environment compared to Elon Musk, for example? The standard person we think about as an influencer is just a person, like Gore, who stands on the stage and tells people to do something else—and they might get some people to take action. But that person has a limited influence and they also go away at some point. It's the Elon Musks who create lasting change. They're the ones changing people's environments to get them to make different decisions.

Another complexity with type one influencers is we can't always see their effect on a system, and it can be difficult to judge how influential it's going to be or in what way. When the Arab Spring was happening in Egypt, for instance, we thought some of the technologies that we now see as a threat to democracy were actually the gateway to democracy.

“The true influencers are the people who are designing the environment.”

Right now it feels like most of the time and resources for invention and innovation are just going toward ways to make more money. Or am I being too dystopian?

I share your general sense that VCs have a short time horizon and they don't like things that take twenty years to create. They like things that take three years to start making money. If you think about what we should be investing in right now, in terms of what's best for all people and the planet, there's no question that we need to put more effort toward things that will take longer to develop. For example, if we can get solar energy right, life will be different. Or solving pollution or challenges with water.

The true influencers are the people who are designing the environment, the people who design supermarkets, the people who are designing gambling, the people who design the little button on Netflix to show you the next video before the previous one has ended. And right now, most of them do seem to be motivated to make more money.

I don't think most of these people consider themselves influencers, by the way, but they are. If you think about how many minutes of other people's lives they impact, the designers behind Facebook are dramatically influential as opposed to the type of person we typically consider an "influencer."

Do you believe effective communication skills are required to achieve influence?

Communication with the people whose behavior you're trying to change isn't key for changing systems, but it is for "type two" influence. For type two influencers, they need to be able to communicate effectively to get people to start changing something. Let's say you come to a talk I'm giving about eating better. I need to convey that issue in a way that gets you to go home and act immediately, because if you wait for a week, your motivation and intentions will go away. Because of that, in my talk I would need to create urgency and a specific idea of what you're going to do—throw away your big plates and get small plates, sign up for a vegetable delivery system, or whatever it is. In this case I'm not trying to change a whole system. What I need to do is to communicate in a way that gets you to be more interested in a particular activity compared to other activities and motivated to implement these changes.

If you want to influence others, is step one giving them an understanding of the systems that create their behaviors?

Helping people understand the system sounds like a good idea, but I don't think it's necessary. Changing the system means getting people to change what they do, not getting them to understand how the system works. Now, from time to time, understanding the system might make the system more appealing and encourage better engagement, but those are rare cases.

In my mind, if I want to influence the world in a scalable way, the right path is to influence the people who build systems. So let's say I get to spend a few days with people who are designing a new credit card. I could say, "Hey, let me help you understand how you can create credit cards that will get people to spend less and save more." That would be influencing the people who could achieve type-one persuasion.

We've talked a lot about changing systems, but how do you actually go about that on a large scale? What does it take to get a government to put new systems in place to shift behavior?

Let me give an example of something that I'm currently engaged with. I recently found, through a lot of data, that the stock of companies that treat their employees well improves much more than the stock of companies that don't treat their employees well. You would think it's obvious, but it's a big deal, and there are specific ways of treating your employees well that actually show up in a company's performance in the stock market. For example, absolute level of salaries don't seem to matter that much, but fairness in salary matters a lot. Quality of furniture and coffee don't seem to matter that much. Transparency of management seems to matter a lot. Inequality in the way companies treat men and women is very damaging.

And so now we're saying, "Okay, we have this finding. How do we get companies to do things differently?" We're trying to figure out if we can pass legislation that would basically force companies to start measuring what we call human capital and report on it in their quarterly and yearly reports. If we can get companies to start measuring and paying attention and reporting, they might also start acting differently.

What I am doing here is trying to create a process that doesn't require people to listen to me and doesn't require people to remember what I've said, and a process that could be continued without me. We just saw the first draft of the law, so it looks like it's moving.

A young person who's moving up in their career wants to become more influential. What advice would you give them?

To be a truly successful type one influencer, someone who designs systems that have a huge amount of impact on the world, it's key to understand the combination of design and human nature. That's true whether you want to design automated thermostats or financial statements or government policies, and it is also a wonderful, exciting way to influence the world.

To be a successful type two influencer, someone who gets on a stage and tells people what to do, you need to find your own voice. Figure out who you're uniquely qualified to reach, with what kind of style, and be consistent in your approach.

In general, I prefer type one influencers over type two, but, from time to time, I need to stand on stage and talk to students or some other audience and try to get people to behave differently. When I do that, I think about who I'm most likely to resonate with and what particular style works for me. I'm a researcher, so my approach is to say, "I'm not superior in any way to the people who are listening. It just so happens that I have been studying this for a while, and my goal here is to tell you what I've been learning. Here's what we know currently about this topic, and here are some of the conclusions you could draw about what we should do next." I think of myself not as someone telling people what to do but as more of a tour guide.

I'm going to give you a billboard that millions of people are going to go by every day. What would you have it say about influence?

Take ownership of your environment
Tweak it for your own benefit

I want people to continuously look at their environment. Don't take it as a given; change it so that it works better for you. Think of something very simple, like the default notifications on your phone. The way phones come out of the box is just not a good setup, right? So don't just live with it. Don't necessarily assume that the environment that you were given is the right one. Figure out what you really want, and spend a bit of time tweaking the environment to get things done in a better way.

EDITOR'S NOTES

Structuring the environment is a hidden but profoundly influential way to shape behavior. See also Moran Cerf's discussion of choice architecture.

> **"Take ownership of your environment. Tweak it for your own benefit."**
>
> **—Dan Ariely**

"The hardest thing I've found in managing people and trying to grow their careers is that everybody wants to focus on their strengths instead of working on their weaknesses."

Dan Bartlett is executive vice president of corporate affairs for Walmart. He is responsible for government relations and public policy, corporate communications, philanthropy, and the company's social responsibility and sustainability initiatives.

Previously, Dan was president and CEO of the US division of Hill+ Knowlton Strategies, where he served as a strategic advisor to business leaders across the American and global economy. Prior to Hill+Knowlton Strategies, Dan was president and CEO of Public Strategies, Inc.

Dan has served in several high-ranking positions at the White House. As one of President George W. Bush's most trusted advisors, he was responsible for all aspects of communication for the president and his administration, including the White House press office, speechwriting, and office of communications.

Dan is a graduate of UT Austin, where he now serves on the advisory board for the College of Communication.

Influential Listening

Dan Bartlett

You've worked for a variety of global leaders, from a US president to Fortune 10 CEOs. From that perspective, how do you define and think about influence?

Influence is the ability to change the behaviors of others. Sometimes that's to the benefit of others, and sometimes you can have a negative influence on people. But the great leaders are those who can change behavior at scale. They can change the behavior of large organizations, of populations.

What do you think enables someone to affect behavior at that kind of scale?

Some of it is communication skills, but it also requires a gift for critical thinking and being able to form persuasive arguments. Take Prime Minister Tony Blair—his ability to articulate his point of view is probably the best I've ever seen.

Tony was always very effective and artful at giving the benefit of the doubt to the other side. Some people try to win a debate by breaking down why the other position is wrong, but he can talk through all sides of an issue and then lead his audience to ultimately understand his point of view. He is very disarming in that regard. There's probably no better training in the art of persuasion than coming up through the British Parliament.

Are there any particular techniques or behavioral patterns you can identify in what makes him (and other global leaders) so effective at influence?

Tony Blair was masterful at knowing his audience, an incredibly complex task considering how varied the audience is for a world leader. The reason this is so important is that when you are trying to persuade somebody, the first thirty to sixty seconds are critical. You can trigger people with the words you choose or just your tonality. I've been in so many situations where I've seen the audience intellectually or even physically shut down on the speaker right out of the gate.

But the other key trait to persuasion is knowing when not to talk. I see that now with my current boss, the CEO of Walmart, the largest company in the world. He's an incredible listener. The most persuasive leaders have an uncanny ability to focus on the person they're talking to in a way that feels uncluttered. They're able to crowd out every piece of noise in the environment and make you really feel like you're the only two people in the world.

Bill Clinton is really good at that as well, as is Josh Bolten, the former chief of staff to President George W. Bush. They're such intense listeners and have an extremely high level of engagement. It's a discipline. It comes more naturally to some, but it's hard to give that kind of devoted attention to someone.

When it comes to influential listening, how much of it is trained versus how much is natural?

I would say it's got to be about 70 percent trained and 30 percent natural. People who are not naturally good at engaged listening can get good at it. One of the traits I see in people who do have a natural inclination for it is a deep sense of curiosity. If you're a curious person, then by default I think you're going to be an incredible listener because you want to investigate a lot of different things, and you want to understand the next level of dimension and depth of how other people think.

You've been in politics as well as business. How different does influence look in these two realms?

Not much. I think the qualities that make for a good leader transfer across politics, business, and culture. There are aspects of those roles and jobs that are very similar anywhere. Walmart has over two million employees and multiple stakeholders. I tell people it's like my second stint in government here. There are a lot of similarities between my old boss and my new boss. The same things make them tick. Their faith, their family, their friends, their ecosystem...

What do you mean by "their ecosystem"?

People who are great leaders and good influencers have a stable and reliable ecosystem in which they operate. Little things like how they manage their schedules, how they perform tasks. There's just an enormous amount of stability in those processes, and that balance affords them the ability to be clear thinkers. Predictability is incredibly important for a leader. People who lead chaotic lives, who are out of balance, just can't lead as effectively.

“Your ability to persuade somebody has to start with being able to hear them.”

That doesn't mean people who are extremely creative and are bouncing around in their lives can't be highly effective. I've just observed that it's less likely.

Now, there's always a time when the most stable leader will surprise people—the exception to the rule. But for the most part, when you're trying to lead large organizations, stability is key. I think we're seeing the proof of that right now with President Trump. The unpredictable nature of the way he leads creates an enormous amount of anxiety, and it's difficult for people to operate in that type of environment.

Look at how President Bush operated during a time when the nation had been attacked. He was trying to persuade the world about the course we were going to take. There had to be an enormous amount of clarity and predictability about where we were heading, given the atmosphere of massive uncertainty, and that informed a lot of our communication strategies.

The same goes in an organization like Walmart. We're in an industry that's being massively disrupted by the Internet. We're trying to take a legacy business and reshape it. And in order to do that with two million-plus employees over twenty-eight countries, you'd better have some predictability as to how you're going to change the organization.

All right, I'm going to ask for your advice. I'm a young person. Let's say I excel at my current job where I'm a heavy individual contributor, but I want to be a leader. What would you tell me do?

You know, the hardest thing I've found in managing people and trying to grow their careers is that everybody wants to focus on their strengths instead of working on their weaknesses. Trying to get people to step out of their comfort zones and work on their weaknesses and take on things that make them feel vulnerable is really important. I was told at a young age by my father that knowing a little bit about everything is probably going to serve you better in life than knowing a whole bunch about one thing. David Epstein's book *Range* strongly reinforces that idea.

I've found that in the younger generation, there's a lot of ambition, and that ambition gets very prescriptive about where they think they should be at certain points. Like, "I should have this kind of role or this job at this point." The result sometimes is they become risk averse. They talk themselves out of taking chances, and when you peel it back you realize it's because they feel like that risk is somehow going to set them back in their career, when in fact calculated risk-taking is one of the most important traits you can develop to become a good leader.

We live in a multidimensional world. Having one really great left tackle is, to me, less important than having a bunch of great athletes who can play multiple positions. So become ambidextrous in your skills. This starts early. For instance, there's such a focus on AI and machine learning for engineers, and kids on that educational track are now almost entirely excluded from the liberal arts. It's to their detriment. Those skillsets are as important as any.

And I would say, finally: be a good writer. We think about being a good presenter and talker and having to stand up and persuade, but at the end of the day the most important art form to me is the written word. It's increasingly a lost art. I can't tell you the number of people I've come across who can't articulate their thoughts or persuade in writing. It's maddening. We have a PowerPoint culture here, and I'm trying to get us to move to a system Jeff Bezos started at Amazon, where you have to write a two- to four-page memo making your case.

One last question: I'm going to give you a billboard. Millions of people are going to see it every day. What would you like it to say about the topic of influence?

Excel at listening.

I think the great influencers are people who are great listeners. I really do. Because ultimately your ability to persuade somebody has to start with being able to hear them.

EDITOR'S NOTES

Like Bartlett, Pohlson also emphasizes the importance of listening for influence—specifically, understanding your audience's priorities before crafting your message.

"Excel at listening."

—Dan Bartlett

"No one likes to be on the receiving end of all these different tactics of the influence process, even if they're applied with a light touch."

Dr. Ethan Burris is a professor of management and the Chevron Centennial Fellow at the McCombs School of Business at the University of Texas at Austin. He is also director of the Center for Leadership and Ethics. He earned his PhD in management from Cornell University and has served as a visiting scholar at Google and Microsoft. He teaches and consults on topics relating to leadership, people analytics, talent insights, managing power and politics, building engagement in teams, and negotiations.

Dr. Burris's research focuses on understanding "employee voice"—getting employees to candidly speak up about problems and opportunities for improvement. In particular, he has investigated how leaders shape employees' decisions whether to speak up or stay silent, and how these voice behaviors influence the performance of the employees who offer their input and the leaders and organizations who receive it.

Activating Employee Voice

Ethan Burris

Your field of study is giving people a voice. How do you think about the nature of influence? How aware are you of the influence you have exerted throughout your career?

Influence fundamentally has to do with change. You have to change something about the way the other person thinks or behaves in the world. And that's what I do for a living. I'm a professor. The point of teaching a class is to have a conversation about a given topic and to help students, executives, whomever, evaluate how they think about that topic and how much they want to change the way they think about it. At the end of a semester, I could reflect back and pump myself up and say, "Yes, I am really influential, because I've done X, Y, or Z, or had this effect on students." But I spend a lot more time on the actual process. What are the ways I could have managed the discussions better? How could I have constructively challenged students' thinking more? I would say I'm more conscious of that, actually, than I am of the outcome.

In terms of teaching, that means understanding how to set up conversations to really surface people's assumptions and then constructively challenge them to rethink their approach. That process is complex and nuanced. Most people go into conversations thinking that they already know a whole lot about the topic. This is especially true with some of the subjects I teach, like leadership and team engagement. Everyone has experiences with leaders and coworkers, after all.

"I'm going to change the way you think about leadership" is a hard conversation to initiate. I have to think about how I can set up the conversations to create that opening, that receptivity that may allow my students to reconsider some of their assumptions.

That process of getting people into a receptive place, whether it be in front of the classroom and instructing students, dealing with departmental colleagues while trying to accomplish things within the school, or talking with my children, is an interesting and fun space to be in.

Do you have a framework for thinking about influence? I like the concept of process, but how do you create it?

My first answer is, well, don't pay any attention at all to *my* framework. There are smarter people out there in the world who've spent their entire careers coming up with the framework of influence and what that process looks like. Some of the factors are, what sort of authority does the person have on the topic? What are the words that come out of their mouth? What's their logic—is it based on a rational, persuasive approach, or is there some emotional appeal involved? There are contextual factors, too, like what's the timing? What are the current political or cultural winds? People like Robert Cialdini and Noah Goldstein have written such excellent books on these frameworks.

Most frameworks do get into the tactics, and I think one risk of overly focusing on tactics is that it can edge toward manipulating other people to behave a certain way. And the thing is, no one likes to be on the receiving end of all these different tactics of the influence process, even if they're applied with a light touch. I don't think the literature talks about that nearly as much as it should.

At the end of the day, if you're talking about the long-term influence process, a lot of the tactics

"'Employee voice' is how we refer to an employee trying to speak up to make changes in an organization."

really start to break down. People don't want to recognize that they've changed because someone had a grand plan in mind to get them to do something different. They want to believe that they've acted in a certain way because doing so is good, just, and ethical, and because it makes sense. Everyone wants to believe that they're acting in a super-logical way. They don't want to realize that they've been manipulated into doing something someone else wants. A lot of the influence process is about bringing the right elements together in such a way that people become receptive to behaving differently than they have before.

In your field of study, in understanding the dynamics of employee voice, have you seen an influence model that you like?

"Employee voice" is how we refer to an employee trying to speak up to make changes in an organization. Almost by definition, it means you're at a lower power position within the organization and trying to make changes to the status quo. The influence process for employee voice is especially challenging because you're asking people who are in charge of your career to take on additional work, make changes to policy that they've often designed themselves, etc. It's an influence process where the deck is stacked against you.

And so, yes, there are frameworks that can help employees be heard. For example, who is speaking up matters a lot. Do they have the credibility to do so? Timing is critical. Communication style matters as well. Are they framing things in terms of dollars and cents, or are they framing things in terms of the cultural values of the organization? You have to factor in who you're pitching to. A successful influence process has to be tailored to each key stakeholder's mindset.

So, in a situation where there's a significant power difference and I am at a power disadvantage, can you offer any tactics or secrets to creating influence within that dynamic?

Most of the work is put in before you sit down and have that discussion. Most successful pitches inside organizations don't happen in a super formal format or within a predetermined, dedicated time. You have to set the table first. Now, how do you do that?

Well one thing is, be selective about when you speak up. You can't be the squeaky wheel all the time. If you speak up about everything, eventually your voice will get discounted. That dynamic doesn't happen with most other influence processes, by the way. If you are a lobbyist and you're trying to get people to go out and vote, speaking up about that on a continuous basis can be a really good thing. But in an organization, if you're routinely speaking up about the vacation policy, eventually people will be inoculated against your voice.

A second thing is to recognize the two main barriers to people engaging in this influence process that are unique to working within organizational hierarchies. One dynamic is that people are very concerned about how risky it is to surface this issue at all. If you are speaking up to the CEO, your immediate boss, or anyone who has real authority over you, then your salary, career trajectory, even your job itself could be at stake. Most people will think twice about taking this risk.

The second dynamic, which is much more fundamental to the influence process, is the probability of success. If you succeed, will people actually make changes in the organization? If you say, "I'm going to challenge my boss about his or her managerial style because it's wreaking havoc on our team," that is a super touchy conversation. It's personal. It's meaningful. And it's really challenging for that manager to hear. Most people think through the likelihood that the boss will be receptive to the feedback. If they expect a negative outcome, they may well choose to stay silent, depriving the company of feedback.

There's a great HBR article called "Getting the Boss to Buy In." It talks about different tactics of issue-selling, offering questions you should consider before starting. I like that framework because—I don't care who you are or what you're trying to influence—there is no one recipe that works for everyone all the time. There are only questions you should be considering, and then you should be adjusting your approach based on a variety of factors. Like, are you likely to generate the right emotions during the process? How, when, where, and to whom should you communicate your message? Are you offering a solution? Are you framing the issue in the right way, whether that's in terms of dollars and cents or cultural values? What's top of mind for your audience? Coming in guns blazing may work very differently from a subtle approach, and which one is better will depend on the organization you're in and the person with whom you are communicating. This framework helps people really think about how safe and worthwhile it is to speak up. And once they evaluate that, they can engage in different tactics to lessen the risk and increase their confidence that their voice will be heard.

Let me give a specific example. Organizations don't just use one type of currency. There are multiple currencies in play all the time. I often use UT as an example of multiple currencies. Any idea that I have, I can pitch in terms of dollars and cents. For instance, "This is something that will drive our costs down, which might in turn drive down tuition costs," definitely resonates with our legislature and the general public. But the university faculty responds to the currency of excellent pedagogy—people are coming here to learn and have life-changing experiences. While cost is an element of that, it's not the driving factor. And a third big currency is the generation of new knowledge. You can't have excellent pedagogy without something to teach.

Around all three of those currencies, there are debates at the lowest and highest levels of the organization. The importance and value of each one may change from year to year depending on other stakeholders, other constituencies. Recognize that there are multiple currencies to be aware of in your field of influence, and that their relative values are fluid. And match those currencies with the stakeholder in question—what faculty care about versus what students care about are different.

Let's say I'm a boss who wants to help rising stars on my team. Do I facilitate their influence from a conversational stream perspective, like with "ask me anything" conversations and town halls, and then simply do what they suggest? Or do I give them more power, for instance with a promotion, so they can better spread their own influence?

By default, anyone who's in a formal leadership position is influential; their influence derives from their positional power. But you don't have to give influence to someone just through a position. If the lowest person in your hierarchy is super passionate about something—fair HR policies, for instance—you don't have to promote them to be VP of HR overnight to get them to engage and enact meaningful change. All you have to do is point to them and say, "These sound like good ideas, and you're really energetic about it. Can you help us put something great together?" Giving someone that opportunity, especially along with resources and political capital to coordinate with others in the organization, can go a long way. All of a sudden you've elevated their status without necessarily elevating their position.

There can be a downside to this. Any time you elevate someone because you think their ideas are great or their heart's in the right place, and you want to give them a bigger platform from which to speak, someone else will come along raising different issues. Elevating someone every time this happens may set up a precedent that's hard to maintain. At some point, people encounter issues that they will need your help, as the leader, to solve. They can't take charge of everything themselves.

If I summarize: power certainly helps with influence, but there are ways to wield influence without power. So power is not necessary for influence.

Absolutely. Take Hong Kong protesting against Chinese legislation that could undermine its autonomy. There is one person, the Chief Executive of Hong Kong, who is fundamentally in charge of deciding what type of legislative issues are going to be considered in their government. But the government is facing massive pushback by a large number of people, spearheaded by a few activists. Now, the chief executive can still retain all that power and give nothing up, but she can also choose to elevate some of the activists into a role where they can help design the language of a new policy. There are ways to be influential without necessarily being the most powerful by title or position.

I'm a young person with big aspirations, and I want to gain more influence in my career. What advice do you have for me?

I guess my first question is, advice for what? What do you want influence over? Once you're clear on that, you need to start with some source of credibility for whatever it is you're trying to be more influential around. Then it's a matter of how you position some of your ideas.

So, if you want to be the most influential person at a university, you'll need to be a reputable academic first, and acquiring that credibility would look very different from acquiring credibility that would set you up to be the CEO of Google. You're not going to be a professor in an academic institution and then run Google, because that's not where the credibility lies. You need the currency that speaks within the organization you are targeting.

As soon as you define what you want to have influence over, then you have to answer the question, why would anyone care about what you think? You need to have something of material value to say. What good will come from the suggestions you are making? After that, you can decide the best way to position some of those ideas so that they resonate better with your target audience, so that you can be influential.

All right, so I'm going to give you a big billboard, Ethan. Millions of people will drive by it every day. What do you want it to say about influence?

Tactics often produce short-lived change.

No one likes to feel like the influence process overrode their logic, so once they have a chance to step back and think about what you're asking them to do, they have to be able to see the good it could achieve. Without a good thought in mind about what it is you want to accomplish and why this change is good, you ultimately won't get people to change. That's where all this has to lead. If your goal is to boost your own status, well, no one wants to follow someone like that. Those people tend to make a less generous impact on the world. So what I'd put on a billboard is, "Influence for what?"

EDITOR'S NOTES

Considering whether someone's argument is based on logic or emotion is something Noah Zandan expands on in his data-driven influence framework.

"Influence for what?"

—Ethan Burris

“Some issues around money involve a very deep-seated fear or concern about how people see themselves and how that self-image is displayed to the public.”

Camera and Naile Photography

Dodee Crockett is a financial advisor with more than three decades of wealth management experience at Merrill Lynch Wealth Management. She has been named to Barron’s annual list of the “Top 100 Women Financial Advisors” for eleven consecutive years and to their list of “America’s Top Advisors: State-by-State” for eight. She has received the Philanthropic Leadership Award (2016) from Baylor Healthcare Foundation and the Spirit of Compassion Award (2008) from Family Compass.

Raised in Dallas and Richardson, Texas, Dodee attended Southern Methodist University. She and her husband, Billy, enjoy supporting acoustic music at their recording studio and give back to the community through their family foundation and work with numerous nonprofits.

Money and Influence

Dodee Crockett

From your perspective and life's work, how do you define the word influence?

To have influence is to be the source of dialog or information that either *confirms* someone's existing opinions, biases, or beliefs or *challenges* them, creating the possibility of change.

I am a financial advisor, and in my field, influence requires credibility. It also requires having authenticity and, I think, a bit of charisma as well—that something special that helps people connect with you. But when it comes down to it, when we say someone is influential in our lives, we often simply mean, "Oh good, this person is someone I can trust, someone I am willing to listen to." They may reflect a confirmation of your own belief or bias and may possibly spur you to take action or change your perspective. The ability to strengthen or alter someone's point of view, that's influence.

Your angle on influence is a unique one. Money, like sexuality and maybe politics, is one of those things that we know are so influential on our lives, yet we don't really talk about it that much.

Talking about money is one of those things that is taboo in our society. You can't walk up to someone and say, "How much money do you have?" I think that having a constructive discussion around money and values is one of the most healthy things I can offer. I want to help people achieve a healthy respect for wealth and a healthy understanding of what wealth can and cannot do.

There are studies that have shown that money can buy happiness to a certain extent. They've quantified this: the optimum annual income to achieve happiness is somewhere between $75 and $90 thousand a year. Based on my experience with clients, I might substitute "a feeling of security" for "happiness." The studies have concluded that above that number, money can become a burden, and below that number, you're striving, maybe struggling.

Most clients feel that if they had just a little bit more money, that would be perfect. It's not a lot more, but it's always just a little bit more. I also hear people talk about the dangers of having too much money. But ultimately, what I have found is that once you get to the point beyond simple security, wealth is not really a burden as long as you are asking good questions about what it means to you and have a spirit of stewardship.

Do you think money itself is influential, or do you think one of the tools of influence is money?

It is absolutely both. Beliefs about money can exert a big influence on someone's life and are shaped by many factors, including family history, peer group, and the media. One person can often hold conflicting beliefs about money without realizing it.

The lack of money, the pursuit of money, and the excess of money are among the most influential factors in life. And since I've seen and worked with people at every position on that spectrum for almost thirty years, it's always been interesting to me to read studies about the relationship between money and happiness, or money and satisfaction.

How have you seen money influence people? How does it motivate behavior?

The way money influences people varies greatly and is sometimes based on how they acquired their wealth. Let's say they are what we would call a self-made person; they tend to have a great respect for what it takes to gain wealth and security.

Those who inherited wealth or grew up with wealth have a very different understanding of money. I don't want to imply that it is always negative. I know that there are many anecdotes about people who have inherited wealth and how those people are entitled and difficult because they don't have a realistic concept of money. But it varies. Yes, there are those who are difficult and entitled, but there are also those who think, "Well I didn't earn this money, but I want to honor the people who did and really make an impact with it."

And then there are the people who had great wealth and then lost it through some circumstance or tragedy. Those people often find it very difficult to adjust themselves to a lesser standard of living.

I've been involved with every one of those life situations. My job as an advisor is to listen to each person's experience and help them find the language to express what they need and gain clarity on their life goals and dreams. I work to help them create a positive image around their resources, money, and wealth so they have a path to move forward.

From your perspective, is money a positive or negative influence on people and their happiness?

On the positive side, when you have money, you have the ability to take action when you're inspired to do so. You can help your family. You can pay for education. Making a difference with money is one of the most fulfilling life experiences that I see.

On the other hand, wealth can bring significant stress and controversy. Once you have wealth, you may get pressure and demands from family or friends. "Invest in my dream," they say. "I've always wanted to own a restaurant—sure, I have no experience with restaurants, but now that you have the ability to make my dream come true, you should do so."

I've seen people lead very difficult lives because of their wealth. Part of that is the stress that an overabundance of anything creates. These people feel like they are targets for every business deal or community charity that is being promoted. Some of them literally go into hiding to protect themselves.

Then there's the pressure to display the trappings of wealth, and frankly that pressure is there whether you have the means or not. The effects of advertising and media on buying habits have been studied for years. It can create divisions within families and stress for individuals.

The list of negatives is fairly long. Listening to these stories and reflecting an understanding of the client's hopes and fears about money takes a real time commitment. Some issues around money involve a very deep-seated fear or concern about how people see themselves and how that self-image is displayed to the public.

You've seen a lot of people make a lot of decisions. If the factors behind each decision could be expressed as one hundred points, how many would be driven by money?

That's really difficult. I know many people who are not motivated by money at all. Some of the people I've worked with over the years would much rather have time and flexibility than money. So, I can't really assign a point value to money. I can only assign a point value to *value*, and that would be pretty much 100 percent.

It's very important for people to understand the hierarchy of values in their lives and to decide what's most important to them. Sometimes that value is money, but not often.

Okay, so our values influence us. Money is obviously a value, time is obviously a value. What other values do you see?

I work with people whose motivation is based on their desire to create something significant; a moral imperative of sharing what they have acquired is a strong value for them. Family is also one, of course. We make decisions all the time based on that. For example, if family is at the top of my value spectrum, I want to work enough so that I can provide for my family—yet if I work too much, then my family doesn't see enough of me. Finding the right balance is the challenge. One of the great discussion points that I have with clients is around what is most valuable to them. We need to determine where money fits on their value scale.

Money is the number one value more rarely than you may expect. People who have experienced scarcity in their life can view money as security, so their highest priority is often something that creates a monetary reward so they can get to a point where they feel secure. If they're choosing between two jobs and one will get them to security faster than the other because the salary is higher, they may decide to select that one. But it's not really about money. It's about security.

It's about what the money means and not about the money itself.

So, money is a means to a value?

Yes.

Though of course for some people it *is* a value. I sometimes say there are people in the world whose entire goal is to stack up their acquisitions in a corner and see how high they can make the pile. I don't feel like those are my best clients. I prefer goals like supporting family, doing something good in society, or finding meaning in one's life.

People may not have the vocabulary for that, but my goal is to help them find it because when they do, they will have a measure of life satisfaction and peace. They will be able to say, "Oh, I did this! I educated my children, did some good with my religious institution, made a real difference to my community." If I can help people translate that value into meaning, to me that's the highest and best use of my work as an advisor.

To paraphrase: We all spend a lot of time thinking about how to acquire money and probably a lot less time thinking about how to connect it to our values and use it well?

That's really my mission. I remember years ago saying to clients, "You're doing so well. But have your children seen the Grand Canyon?" They were so wrapped up in the acquisition of money that I just wanted to call it out to them. I said, "Let's have this journey mean something. Let's create experiences. You may not remember the acquisition of this money, but you will remember that trip to the Grand Canyon with your children."

If I can help direct the influence of money in the most positive direction, then I've done my job.

There's a study that looked at the differences in people's willingness to collaborate and be friendly and easy to work with before and after they have power. It found that nice people who suddenly gain power do change their behavior. Does wealth work the same way? If I suddenly acquire it, does that change who I am? Does it change my values, my identity?

Honestly, I don't know how it could *not* change your identity to some extent. Let's say you were working hard to gain security and now you suddenly have security. Not only do you have security, but you have an excess of security. What do you do with that? I think we've all seen evidence of people who, when they achieve sudden wealth, don't have a concept of how to steward it. Stewardship is a key concept in dealing with money. We all know the story of the people who won the lottery and three years later were back to working in fast food. It was because they had no preparation for or assitance in stewarding their resources.

You could give someone a million dollars and they'd think, "I'm rich! I'll go buy a house for nine hundred thousand dollars." But then they can't afford to keep that house because they don't have a concept of the difference between the cost of buying something and the ongoing cost of maintaining something.

Then there are also those who say, "Wow I have this newfound wealth. I'm not going to do anything with it for a while because I need to think about how best to use it. I need to gather around me the people who can help me be thoughtful about the next move." Those are the people who are changed by their wealth for the better. There's no one real path for this. What I hope for people in that situation is that they surround themselves with good, competent advisors who help them ask the right questions.

Someone said to me when I was very young that the quality of your life is determined by the questions you ask yourself. I live by that. I'm always asking, is this a good thing? Questioning doesn't mean that you are wishy-washy. It means that you always want to make sure you are challenging complacency so that you stay on the path that reflects your values.

Let's say that I want to have influence, and I take a path of acquiring money to achieve that influence. Do you see those things as connected, and what counsel would you give me?

I feel like influence has a lot more to do with authenticity than money. I mean, I find myself far more influenced by people who live authentic lives,

“Someone said to me when I was very young that the quality of your life is determined by the questions you ask yourself.”

people who volunteer, who may not have great wealth but who are passionate and active in their passion. That doesn't require great wealth.

When I'm working with people, especially young people, I'm trying to help them find a way to acquire enough wealth that they feel secure. I want them to know their basic resources are intact so that they can make decisions from a place of confidence and safety. They need enough safety so that a setback, for example a lost job, doesn't take them off track. It would mean they can afford to look for the next *right* position, not just the next job.

The most important initial goal is to get to the point where your decisions are not based on fear for your own or your family's well-being.

Money is a means to an end.

Absolutely. Remember that in the long run, money is a servant, it is not your master. But you have to treat your money like you would treat good servants. In other words, you wouldn't ask the servants to risk their lives to work for you. You would be prudent about caring for them. If you want your money to serve you for a long time, you must treat it well, but it should not be what controls you.

Your values are ultimately what control you, and once you've reached a level of safety, then we're exploring values, not acquisition. We've seen it many times where people who made the choice to follow their passion turned that into something that was lucrative and created great wealth. So, it's not an either/or. I would love for everyone to find something they are passionate about, that also provides a level of comfort and safety and self-regard.

Let's say I'm a young person, and I want to gain influence by doing things I'm passionate about. What advice would you have for me?

Volunteer for something, and be good at it. If you are passionate about a particular issue, go be part of the solution for that issue—show up. Be there every time. I had this experience with a young person years ago who had been granted an internship in a highly competitive field. I said to him, "You need to be sitting at the door when the person comes to unlock it in the morning, and you need to be willing to do the things that need to be done, and you need to be there until they lock the door at night. During this time, observe and be friendly. Volunteer for the jobs that no one wants."

And in the end, he was hired three months later. They put him on the full-time payroll. This was a very unusual situation, but in general, that level of passion, work ethic, and connectivity pays off. Many times people will say to themselves, "I'll sign up to help with this organization, and then if I make it to the meeting, great, but if I get a better offer, I'll do that instead. I'll just send my regrets and a promise to make it next time." But real influencers are always present.

Influence is something you earn. Be good at what you do. Be there when you say you will. Contribute real ideas, and show your passion.

I'm going to give you a billboard that millions of people are going to drive by every day. What do you want that billboard to say about influence?

For me, it would say something about the importance of asking questions. Whether I'm trying to influence someone or someone is trying to influence me, some of the questions are always, Who will benefit from the outcome? Does it reflect my values? And then, am I ready to act? Questioning like that is, to me, key to every part of life. Maybe that's my billboard.

Ask good questions. Then, be ready to act.

EDITOR'S NOTES

Putting your audience first is key to influence, and a big part of that, according to Crockett and many other contributors, is understanding what they value.

"Ask good questions. Then, be ready to act."

—Dodee Crockett

“Access to the right data is incredibly liberating and empowering.”

Brett Hurt began programming at age seven, doing so online at age eighteen. He is now the CEO and cofounder of data.world, a Public Benefit Corporation (and Certified B Corporation®) that is an enterprise data catalog for corporations and organizations as well as the world's largest collaborative data catalog and community. Brett co-owns Hurt Family Investments (HFI) with his wife, Debra. HFI is involved in seventy-seven startups, twenty-one VC funds, and dozens of philanthropic endeavors.

Brett cofounded and led Bazaarvoice as CEO through its IPO, follow-on offering, and two acquisitions. Bazaarvoice became the largest public SaaS business in social commerce. Brett also founded and led Coremetrics, which was rated the #1 Web analytics solution by Forrester Research and acquired by IBM.

In 2017, Brett was given the Best CEO Legacy Award by the Austin Business Journal. His book, *The Entrepreneur's Essentials*, is available free of charge at medium.com/@databrett.

Patrick McGarry is currently building the thriving data community around data.world as the head of strategic partnerships. He has worked to build communities and foster Open Source ideals at companies like Sourceforge/Slashdot, Alcatel-Lucent, and Perforce. Patrick served as the Director of Community for the Ceph open source project at the startup “Inktank,” and later for Red Hat after a successful acquisition.

Patrick enthusiastically helps companies understand and adopt Open Source ideals through community engagement, conferences, and events, and he continues to be a strong advocate of FOSS on the desktop and in the enterprise.

Democratizing Data

Brett Hurt & Patrick McGarry

How do you both define the word influence?

PATRICK: In this day and age, I think about influence as your ability to have an impact on the character development of an industry, an ecosystem, or an idea, and on the people who interact with it—whether they're customers, employees, partners, investors or some other stakeholder group.

BRETT: I agree with all of that. I would also say that influence is when you're trying to get someone to take an action or learn something new or change their perspective. Sometimes it can even be reinforcing something they already know.

PATRICK: How we think about influence has changed a lot since the early days of Tony Robbins. We have a whole new noun: "influencer." The fact that it's a full-time job now really reflects how influence has evolved, and we are learning what it can do, for good or for ill.

You deal with the intersection of data and influence. Tell me about it.

PATRICK: It's important to recognize that data can be leveraged for influence. Some companies, like Google and Facebook, have a huge amount of data. They can and do use this data to influence behavior. By contrast, companies that we might consider data "have-nots" are often so far behind the power curve that they have to build influence before they can use the data they do have.

BRETT: I've been on a journey since I was twenty-six, trying to influence people to see the truth about their businesses. If I go back to my Coremetrics days, the majority of online businesses were flying

“Historically, how people have used data is that one or two very smart people would go off into their dark corner and perform some complex incantations and come back with insight.”

blind without access to good data or metrics. This meant they were often wasting massive amounts of time every week.

One of the stories I remember is from Eddie Bauer. They would spend four hours every Monday debating the hero image on their homepage. Using data, we were able to show them that only 5 percent of people ever clicked on that hero image, and less than 2 percent of those made a purchase. So they just stopped investing their time in it. This had been a natural behavior for them as a cataloger by heritage. I saw first-hand that access to the right data is incredibly liberating and empowering.

Data is making a huge impact on how businesses operate, and I get a big kick out of that. When big, iconic, hundred-year-plus companies like L.L.Bean stand up on stage like they did during my BazaarVoice days and say, "We have completely transformed the way we handle products because of data," you know you've influenced behavior. Now, when they get a certain number of negative reviews, they do one of three things: in option one, which is the vast majority of cases, they improve the product. In option two, if the product has utility but they don't want to sell it again, they donate it to charity. Under option three, which is exceedingly rare, they eliminate the product altogether.

You can see how data can be enormously influential in getting people to be more efficient and to design whole new processes. Successful online businesses already have metrics that reinforce strong accountability. In the future, any business without good data will struggle.

What factors do you think create influence as you just defined it?

BRETT: People are all at various stages of searching for truth. The more perspective, experience, and data you have, and the more you're leveraging the data, perspective, and experience of others, the more likely you are to be both influenced and influential. This is because most people want to know the truth. We're wired that way. If you go back to the original tribal days, people who didn't band together and support each other by sharing information and resources simply didn't survive.

Now, a lot of us in the knowledge economy are working in air-conditioned buildings with free snacks, so it's not a matter of life and death, but information still determines critical events like elections. It can also be life or death for a business—corporate death.

At an Aspen Action Forum event I attended, Walter Isaacson said his biggest takeaway in studying the amazing leaders he biographed is that they were all incredible collaborators—that we, as human beings, are natural collaborators and that is the trait most responsible for our prosperity.

PATRICK: I think information can still mean literal life or death. Especially in the time of fake news and this downward spiral into visceral responses, when the gulf between the haves and the have-nots is so vast. The people using data to influence the world are able to understand and aggregate this sophisticated picture and drive other people to action, often without their knowledge.

BRETT: There are enormously powerful data technologies, such as knowledge graphs, that Amazon and Google and Facebook use, and most people just have no idea what they are, let alone how to use them. One of my great sources of pride in data. world is that we're democratizing access so that the have-nots have a lot more useful data, and access to much more powerful data technologies, than they otherwise would. For instance, we're making it easy to understand and utilize knowledge graphs, which our Fortune 500 customers use inherently on our platform. But companies without their own army of data scientists have never had the capability to do so before now.

Could you explore the concept of democratizing data access through the lens of influence? If data is influential because it's a lens to the truth, help me understand how democratizing data supports that.

BRETT: Take millennial knowledge workers today. They were raised on Google and Wikipedia. They're used to having instant access to information. When they work inside companies built with antiquated tools and unsophisticated tropes around data management, when it's all about data governance and locking things down, keeping things on premise, it's the exact opposite of what these workers are accustomed to in their daily lives.

There's a power center in these companies, which tends to be very small and IT-led. And the millennials are like, "Where's the data to do my job? Where's the data about how the business is performing?" It's very hard for them to get access to it. Then compare that to a company like Airbnb, whose fifth employee was a data scientist: they've had an internal data catalog since close to the beginning of the company, and now over half of their employees use it. It's one of the most successful companies in the history of travel. That's what the Fortune 500s are up against.

Our vision is that it should be super easy to catalog data and manage permissions so that employees have access to the data they need to do their jobs. That will give employees enormous amounts of influence in the company because they actually know the truth about the business and the various aspects that they're working on. They will have the capability to make faster and better decisions.

A lot of times, the tools simply don't exist yet. We're evolving from a command-and-control hierarchy to a much more distributed, decentralized organization. We're in this business transition where data is the new oil, but the reality is that, inside many companies, data is buried deep in its crude state, not refined, and very hard to find and access.

It's really cool when one of these companies turns the lights on across the business, unleashing influence all over the company. What leaders should care about is not just releasing or democratizing influence among the leadership ranks. That's important, but it should really be among their whole team—the book *Tribes* by Seth Godin laid this out eloquently.

PATRICK: Historically, how people have used data is that one or two very smart people would go off into their dark corner and perform some complex incantations and come back with insight. A lot of times that insight was missing context that you might get from people who weren't as data-technical. One thing that data.world, and the data ecosystem in general, needs to do is get more people involved in that data conversation earlier.

So you've got subject matter experts, you've got the people in the field that can say, "Hey, this number that you came up with doesn't look right based on what I see every day." It's about having more people at the table in a way that is very collaborative. We work with one group called the Ocean Data Alliance. It's part of the UN and does a lot of work on oceanic sustainable development goals. It brings together ocean researchers from across the globe to have conversations and share data in a powerful way that's never been done before.

One of my favorite books of recent history is Doug Laney's *Infonomics*. He talks about the economics of data and how, yes, you can operationalize your data, which most people should do but don't do a very good job of. Yes, you can even monetize your data directly, but there are a lot of other things in between. One thing that he highlights very specifically is using data as currency. I think as the data ecosystem and the data economy evolve over the next five to ten years or so, we're going to see data as its own sort of currency when it comes to conversations between organizations. That's a whole level of influence that we haven't even begun to explore.

BRETT: One interesting point. In 2017, the most popular dataset on data.world was put together by a citizen data scientist on the Russian propaganda effort leading up to the presidential election. The *Washington Post* and the *New York Times* both wrote about and linked to that dataset. That was interesting from an influence standpoint. Also, we ran an analysis of how data influences the news. We did a pretty broad-based survey across the political spectrum. Everyone from very conservative to very liberal people said that having easy access to the data behind a news article would significantly increase their trust in that news.

Nancy Duarte's book *Data Story* talks about how the necessary competency for data is actually your ability to tell a story around it, not just your ability to access and manipulate it. Going back to your perspective on the factors of influence, how do you think about data as a liberating source of truth while addressing the fundamental competency you need to deliver it?

PATRICK: There's a site called datapractices.org that we built to address this issue. We realized very early on with data.world that there was a lack of general data literacy. So we spent a fair bit of time and effort with the broader data community building a resource to address that. We had a data science leadership summit where we got together some visionary folks across data science, semantics, and open source and facilitated discussions about state-of-the-art practices within various data communities.

We realized that there were a lot of common threads between how software development evolved and how data was evolving. We wanted to use lessons learned from software development to help move people forward, build a common lexicon, and get people up to speed faster. We started with a data practices manifesto, which was our response to the agile manifesto. But the agile movement only took off because there was an army of consultancies saying, "Here, I'm going to show you how to be agile."

It was always our intent to go beyond just words on a page, which we've done now. We've built OpenCourseWare and moved it all under the umbrella of the Linux Foundation. It's a neutral third party now. That means anyone can participate and contribute content. Organizations like Chart.io, dataliteracy.com, Oracle, and Microsoft have contributed content. We want the community to be self-educating and able to help each other.

We've found that education can be hugely influential. We show people, "Here's how you can get a handle on building a data-driven culture in your organization, even if you can't write a single line of code." It's been a very rewarding project and continues to grow.

Let's say I'm a young person building my career. I want to be more influential—maybe not an influencer, but I want to be more influential as a leader. What advice would you give me?

BRETT: I would say it's very, very important to build up your data skills even if you're not going to be a data scientist per se. If you've got a proclivity toward math and programming, you would have a much easier time getting a great career in data science then even in computer science these days. The nation has a huge dearth of these people. If you're also good at presenting and have data storytelling skills, then you could become incredibly influential. Companies are desperate for people like you to join and create change inside of their organizations. They must do that to evolve, or they really will die out.

There are lots of tools available now. There's the data practices courseware, which Patrick was talking about, and tons of programs at places like Galvanize and General Assembly. Alternatively, getting a master's degree in data science is not a bad idea.

Back in the early 2000s I was trying to convince students to go into software-as-a-service. That turned out to be a lucrative career trajectory. Now I think that over the next ten or twenty years, it will be people with data skills who will be highly influential in companies and have incredible careers.

PATRICK: I think the biggest thing about building a career is being multidisciplinary. A lot of times people tend to be very focused. They get a business degree or they get a computer science degree, but I think we're moving past the time when you can be just one thing. I think you need to have broader understanding. You need to be able to interact with other groups and, more importantly, be able to translate what's going on between those two groups.

Even if you're not super technical, being a really savvy data consumer who can then translate that into multiple settings is going to be extremely powerful. Being a data storyteller is going to be extremely important regardless of your role. That's my broad-stroke advice for having an influential career: be a good data storyteller.

I want to wrap with one final question here. I'm going to give each of you guys a billboard. Millions of people are going to drive by it every day. What would you like that billboard to say on the topic of influence?

BRETT: Data is liberating.

PATRICK: I want to combine that with encouraging people to get savvier about data. Not for business acumen, but simply for the ability to make informed decisions for themselves. That's missing from our society right now, that ability to dig deeper into the data and be informed consumers. I don't know what the billboard would say, exactly, but definitely something about how the power is in the data. You just have to dig deeper.

BRETT: How about "Data is liberating. The truth is out there if you dig deeper."

EDITOR'S NOTES

For many, data is the most important influencer. On the other hand, Heather Berlin points out that much of our behavior is driven by hidden often unconscious factors.

"Data is liberating. The truth is out there if you dig deeper."

—Brett Hurt & Patrick McGarry

“People fail to recognize, by a long shot, the influence they have over others by simply asking for something.”

Vanessa Bohns is an associate professor of organizational behavior at Cornell University. She holds a PhD in social psychology from Columbia University and a BA in psychology from Brown University. Her research on social influence and compliance has been published in top academic journals in psychology, management, and law, and has been featured in *The New York Times, The Wall Street Journal, New York Magazine, Forbes, Fast Company*, and on NPR's “Here and Now.” At Cornell, she teaches courses on organizational behavior, morality and ethics, and negotiations.

You Are Already Influential

Vanessa Bohns

How would you describe what you study to a layman?

I study people's beliefs about their influence over others. People regularly try to determine the impact of their words, actions, and presence on others—and regularly get it wrong, but not in the way you might think. People almost always underestimate their influence.

I learned this lesson personally as a graduate student. During a project I worked on with a Columbia Business School professor, I was required to collect data by going up to strangers in New York's Penn Station and asking them to fill out surveys. Each time I approached someone, I braced myself for rejection. However, rejection came far less often than I anticipated. When I approached people individually and face-to-face, I had so much more influence than I realized. And now I've watched my own study participants come to the same realization for fifteen years.

How do you assess the influence we actually have as opposed to the influence we think we have?

In a typical study, my participants have to ask people—usually complete strangers—to perform an action such as donate to charity, hand over their phone, vandalize a library book, or tell a lie. Before they leave the lab, I ask participants to guess how many people will say yes to their request, and then they go on to record how many people actually do say yes or no. So, it's a matter of comparing their expectations to the results.

My studies have logged more than 15,000 individual requests. Consistently, participants

underestimate the number of people they can get to agree to their requests by about 50 percent. They fail to recognize, by a long shot, the influence they have over others by simply asking for something.

Can you give some examples of how this shows up in daily life? What should we watch out for?

People misperceive their own influence in all sorts of contexts. We think sending an email is roughly as effective as asking for something face-to-face, when it is in fact much less effective. We think we should ask our friends for things when strangers are nearly equally likely to agree. We think we should ask someone who said "yes" to us previously, when someone who said "no" is actually more likely to agree to a follow-up request. And, importantly, we think others feel more comfortable than they do saying "no" to our inappropriate requests.

These misperceptions lead us to misjudge our influence over others and to wield the influence we do have in suboptimal ways.

What advice do you have for a smart, driven person who wants to be more persuasive and influential in the "real world"? What advice should they ignore?

What my studies have taught me about influence is this: Ignore all the advice on how to be more influential. Instead, become more aware of the influence you already have on others every day.

You have much more influence than you think.

EDITOR'S NOTES

Many contributors to this volume began their careers by first noticing, and then developing, the influence they already had.

"You have much more influence than you think."

—Vanessa Bohns

"Other people are the main driver of almost every decision that people make in their lives."

Gil Eyal is the CEO and founder of HYPR, the award-winning market leader in data-driven influencer marketing automation solutions. Gil has revolutionized the way many of the world's biggest agencies and brands are running influencer marketing by focusing on the same data, analytics, and audience demographic information that's relevant to traditional digital marketing.

A pioneer in the influencer space, Gil also served as the COO of early player photo-sharing app Mobli Media and has worked with influencers ranging from Nash Grier and Cameron Dallas to Leonardo DiCaprio, Pitbull, and Serena Williams.

Gil was the 2017 recipient of the Digiday Top Boss Award in the technology industry and is a two-time winner of the MarCom Awards for Excellence in Marketing and Communications. He has an MBA from the Kellogg School of Management at Northwestern University and a Bachelor of Laws from Bar-Ilan University in Israel.

Insights from the Influencer Marketplace

Gil Eyal

From your perspective running an influencer marketplace, how do you define the term influence?

At the very basic level, influence is just the ability to cause somebody else to do something. That could be as small as changing their opinion or as big as getting them to make a life-affecting decision.

Almost every decision we make is influenced by somebody. As human beings, we're actively seeking people to influence our decisions. Where to eat, which movie to see, whether to go on a second date with that girl, which college to attend. If you look back at your life, you'll see that there were specific people you consulted with, or maybe you looked at what they did as an example, in order to make many of your decisions.

Other people are the main driver of almost every decision that people make in their lives. Traditional channels of influence like branding or advertising have become less and less effective for a variety of reasons. So influence that's integrated into and relevant to our everyday life, especially for younger generations, has taken a much bigger role.

Having evolved influence from a concept to an item with economic value, what are the factors that make someone influential?

I think the number one thing is being perceived as somebody who's worth listening to. In childhood, often that's our parent or teacher, or maybe an older kid from our neighborhood that we admire. And then later on in life, that someone could be a colleague or a mentor, or someone you recognize as having expertise in a particular space. "Oh, this guy really knows technology. I can ask him about which phone I should buy." Or, "I know this person travels a lot. They'll tell me how to get the cheapest flight or the best seat."

Those relationships grow from simple connections—they're just part of your circle or they're your superior at work. To you, they are simply the people you think of when you're making a choice. You are thinking, "Who are the people that I admire and who will help me shape my decisions, my thought processes?" Over the last few years, we've been seeing people actively work to become those whom others choose to give influence over their decisions.

Why do you think people want to be influencers?

I think it's human nature, right? Forget all the benefits that you can earn by being considered influential and somebody who's a thought leader. It's human nature to want to be respected for what you do. Now, once you've got that, people want to look for the benefits that come from it, whether it's political gain, financial gain, being promoted at work, or getting bigger clients because you're considered an opinion leader. This is nothing new. What's new is that today we can measure that influence, and access to the channels of influence has changed. Today you can just start your own media channel.

If I want to actively be more influential, what do you recommend that I do?

Well, it's a combination of things. First, you have to specialize. It's very hard to be influential across everything. Yeah, Justin Bieber has a big audience, but he's not influential when it comes to buying books about poker. There are people who are experts on poker, and they have a very specific poker audience that listens to and respects their advice a lot more than Justin Bieber saying, "Oh, this is a great poker book, you should buy it."

Second, you have to get your message out there. So create content or engage with people in a way that demonstrates the value that your knowledge can create for them. You have to be generous with that knowledge. It's very different from the old-school model of, "Let me charge you a hundred bucks an hour to sit with me, and then I'll share that knowledge." Today it's more like, "I'm giving out my knowledge as part of my social presence, and I'll gain in other ways."

When you're generous enough with your expertise that people know about it, they start to share it, and you gain that new following. It's a virtuous cycle, where the bigger the expert you are, the more content you share, the more other people will share it, and the bigger the following you have; and then the next time you share content, you'll start with a bigger circle of people passing it on. The people who know how to do this really well, really benefit from it—we're not necessarily talking Kim Kardashian here, but maybe the person who does Kim Kardashian's makeup.

How much do you think the motivation to be influential is financial versus what I'll call clout?

There's this image that riches and fame go together, which isn't necessarily true. There are a lot of people who have a big following online and have not found ways to monetize that successfully. But because of that pervasive image, there's almost an epidemic of people treating themselves as businesses and looking for ways to make money. It's kind of a new version of the American dream, right? Of finding riches and fame through doing what you love to do and having a lot of opportunities to do it. Being an influencer is just a way to get there. Pretty much anyone can be an expert on anything and build an audience now.

Okay, so I want to get back to something you said earlier about measurement. You run an influencer marketplace: how do you measure influence?

The industry itself suffers from a willingness to settle for metrics that don't really measure influence. They measure attention, but for this industry to really become big, it needs to shift away into performance-based metrics. What happens when this person promotes a product? Do people end up buying it? And that's a question that isn't being answered very well today by the different providers in the space.

Right now, there's this general idea that the clout and the fame of the people I work with will bring benefits to my brand. That's very different than saying, "Okay, I paid a thousand dollars, but I quantify the value at three thousand. I got a good return on my investment." The ability to quantify the ROI informs and pushes decisions through. It's one thing to say, "Look, we did this, and we got a lot of likes, and it was great." It's much more powerful to say "Look, this was ROI positive for us, so can you approve a bigger budget?"

Influence, at the end of the day, is the ability to drive people to make decisions or drive them to take action, and until influencers are forced to demonstrate that they can produce those results, the industry's going to be limited.

Is influence ultimately trackable, though? Or is it this ideal thing that's far away, and while we might be good at measuring reach, we're nowhere near being ready to measure what changes as a result of that reach?

I think it's absolutely trackable, and it's coming. I'll say we just received a patent in the influence-tracking space—it's not the only solution, but it's a definite step forward. In general, we're going to see a whole different language around influencers evolve in the next year or so. It's not going to be focused on likes and shares; it's going to be focused on digital marketing language. What was your conversion rate? How many people ended up buying? What was your CPM? What was your CPC?

And what we'll see is that the question of whether or not influence can convert to behavior change will vary from influencer to influencer. It will separate the truly influential ones from those who just have the ability to draw a lot of attention. When that separation happens, we'll see a shift in the way people think about influencers, where potentially the Justin Biebers and Kim Kardishians of the world will no longer be the most sought-after influencers. It will be the ones who provide a return that makes sense for brands and that can be compared apples-to-apples to other channels.

The metrics you're stating there remind me a lot of what you'd look at elsewhere, maybe in e-commerce. But we're talking about people here, not clicks. It leads to the question, can influence be bought?

Expertise is very hard to manufacture. The ability to be considered an expert has to have something real behind it. People always refer to it as authenticity. You're not going to say things that are obviously irrelevant to people who know the space. Of course you can be the biggest expert in the world, but nobody knows about it, and *visibility* can be purchased. It can be purchased in the traditional way of buying media exposure, doing PR, or by collaborating with people who reach the audience you want.

Let's take Dr. Oz as an example. If he was never on Oprah, he'd just be another doctor. He'd still be an expert. He just wouldn't be nearly as influential.

And what does it mean to buy an audience? It's not how big your audience is, it's how that audience views you. Followers are not all equal. I follow Aerosmith. I loved Aerosmith when I was younger. I still listen if a song comes up on Apple Music, but I definitely don't view them as anybody who shapes any decision in my life. That wasn't true twenty years ago when I dressed how you would expect an Aerosmith fan to dress. The biggest challenge in the influencer space is to stop looking at likes and shares and instead try to understand the emotion behind them.

Let's say your cousin is a singer. You're probably going to do everything you can to support what they do; you'll follow them, and you'll share every piece of content because the nature of your relationship is much stronger than it would be with an artist that you just happen to like. Same thing if you follow Kim Kardashian's makeup person: you might admire them so much that every single piece of advice they give is something that you pay attention to. The strength of that follow is much, much stronger than say, my Aerosmith follow. And that's a big challenge, because yes, a lot of people have a lot of followers. But how important is that relationship to the follower? Does that follower view the connection as more than just, "Okay, I clicked on a button a few years ago"?

Tell me more about how authenticity operates in the influencer marketplace world.

Influential people have to maintain authenticity. It has to be natural. If you're changing who you are in order to gain visibility in this influence world, you're going to get called out. We're at the point where content gets pushed out very quickly and it's seen by a lot of people, some of whom are experts in the space. They have the ability to respond immediately. Authenticity is more than a requirement to produce good content. Of course there's always the odd exception, but broadly speaking, if you're not authentic then you will be demolished online.

If you claim to be an expert on a subject and you say the wrong things, that's going to come out very quickly. It's much easier to lose influence than to generate it. There's not a lot of room for mistakes.

How do you mesh the desire for authenticity with brands that want to buy influence? I follow somebody who's influential about fashion, but then all of a sudden I see her in sponsored ads and know that she's getting paid to market some piece of clothing that she may or may not like.

We recommend that people don't go for the old-school tactic of, "Okay, here's a pretty face; let's put our clothes on her and then share it on social." We recommend they take a much deeper dive into what kind of audience they have and the nature of their relationship with the prospective influencer. On our platform, we don't really care about follower count. We care about the conversations followers are participating in and what's happening when they talk about a subject.

Let's take Kate Upton. She was the face of Bobbi Brown Cosmetics a few years ago, and she has

"The influencer marketplace is a self-policing ecosystem. If someone sells out, somebody else quickly takes their place."

a beautiful face. In the '80s or '90s, that's all you needed. But she has a 90 percent male following. The people she reaches aren't the ones who care about cosmetics.

There's a lot of planning and analytics dedicated to understanding whether somebody's actually going to be able to effectively communicate the message that you want to send. We strongly recommend looking at the people *next* to the celebrities and superstars, looking at the people who support them. If it is a beauty brand or a fashion brand, look at their stylists, their makeup artists. Those people are going to be far more authentic when they talk about why they like your product because they'll be able to say, "I like this product because it's organic. It stays on for this long. I use it on myself, and I'm an expert in this space."

It's kind of a self-policing ecosystem. If someone sells out, somebody else quickly takes their place. They have to be really careful and do some due diligence on every product they get involved with, or they will pay a price for it. It's the same with brands.

Our advice to influencers is not to promote something they don't believe in. Our advice to brands is not to work with influencers who don't believe in their products. If they're positioned as an expert and they really believe in it, then that's going to come across as very authentic even though the content might be sponsored.

Are there any markers of authenticity that you've discovered?

It's one of those things where you don't know it till you see it.

"It's human nature to look to others to help us make our decisions."

There are some signals, like if the person genuinely uses the product regularly. So we always tell brands, "Do not do one-time engagements. If you're going to work with an influencer, do an annual deal with them and have them be featured all the time. Show them using your product all the time. And make them make a real sacrifice. If they hate your product, then they're going to suffer with it for a whole year." And audiences are looking for that. If an influencer mentions something and then never uses it, the audience remembers.

So there's no direct measurement ahead of time, but afterward, there's definitely performance measurement. Did this lead to sales? Did this lead to additional engagement on our website? Did people sign up for a demo? Those are metrics you could look at and say, "Okay, this was clearly an effective engagement."

Can I ask how much the average campaign costs? For example, I want to buy an influencer to move some topic forward. What's the average going rate for that?

It obviously varies greatly based on who's asking. If you're a nonprofit, you get it for free. If you're Nike, you could get it for shoes. If you're an unknown brand, you might have to pay more. There's a general industry pricing thing that says that for every 10,000 followers, you should get about a hundred dollars per campaign. Somebody who has a million followers would get about $10,000.

We've seen a very interesting scenario in the space, where as you go down from the really big influencers to the smaller influencers, a lot of promotions either happen for free or are not really promotions—they're just the influencer promoting something on their own in order to appear like they have campaigns. There's an enormous amount of that. It's kind of a "the chicken or the egg" scenario. Who's going to give you a campaign if you've never done a campaign before?

So, do you consider yourself to be an influencer?

In certain contexts, everybody's an influencer. I'm somewhat of an influencer in the influencer marketing space. There are probably a few hundred people that follow me on social media that care about influencer marketing, and I influence their thoughts about it. I influence the way my son thinks about things. I happen to be a big gaming nerd, so there are a few friends who want to buy their kids an Xbox or a PS4 who might ask me what to buy, so I have some influence there. If you think about yourself, there are some situations where people will turn to you and ask you what to do about something because you're the one who knows about it.

It's human nature to look to others to help us make our decisions. Decisions are made by learning and gathering information from the environment around us, and going to people you trust is a much healthier way to collect that information than through ads or promotional content.

Are people more trustworthy than ads at least partly because we know the intent of ads and promotional content, and we don't like it?

Partly, but there's also just a bombardment of ads. Do you remember the last ad you saw online? No, because no one does. I sit in front of rooms of hundreds of people and I ask, "Who here remembers the last ad they saw?" And about 2 percent of people will remember the ad, but they won't remember the brand. If they do remember the brand, a lot of times they're upset because they know exactly why they were targeted. They're like, "How do they know this? Are they reading my conversations? Are they listening to me?"

We are being programmatically fed ads trying to get information about us so the advertisers can then push these ads at us in a promotional way, and of course we become blind to them and install technology to block them. The result is that programmatic marketing in the United States will be a hundred-billion-dollar business in 2019. A hundred billion.

A while back I put Adblocker Plus on my browser, and then I went on to major websites and saw how many ads were being blocked. The average news site in the United States has thirty or forty ads on its homepage. It's not consumable, and you know how that happened? They used to have one, and people would click on it, and they would make X dollars. And then fewer people clicked, so they said, "Okay, let's put two ads up." And that worked for a while, until it didn't, and then they said, "Why don't we also make them pop up? Hide them in the text? Make them hard to close?"

I want to ask for your advice. I'm a young person starting my professional career, and I want to be influential in an authentic way. I have something that I care about. What would you recommend that I do?

The number one thing is to ensure that you become really, really knowledgeable. Be really, really good at something. We no longer live in a society that rewards generalists.

And then the second thing is, start generating content around the thing you're good at. When you get discovered, start matching with other people with similar interests and creating content with them. Because we mentioned the two components of influence today are having real expertise and getting it out there. My advice would be to take it away from the social media environment. If you're an intern at a company, and you're an expert on a subject because your entire life you've been coding or playing video games, and your social media followers know that but the CEO of your company doesn't? Well, then there's no value in your expertise. You're never going to stand out—you're going to be one of twenty interns.

You have to find ways to get that knowledge out there. You're not going to knock on the CEO's door and say, "Hey, by the way, I know how to program." But you also want to make sure, when it comes up, that they're aware of it. That's how you generate opportunity for yourself. So, the same thing with online content. You want to start creating so that when people Google your name, they'll see, "Hey, this guy has done a few things in this space."

You want to create content and put it in the right places. You could put beauty videos on Instagram and YouTube. If it's gaming you might want to go to Twitch. Be in the right place, and start creating content that'll show people you know what you're talking about. Sometimes people get really lucky and get discovered overnight, but most of the time, it's a grind. You have to put in a lot of work to stand out.

I'm going to give you a billboard that millions of people are going to see every day. What do you want that billboard to say about influence?

If my target audience is marketers, I would say, "Remember that marketing fundamentals still apply to influencer marketing." So, targeting—I know I'm explaining my own billboard now—but targeting, segmentation, measurement, all those things have to happen. This industry's been very, very minimalist about focusing on those things.

If the audience is broader, I have a much bigger, world peace-type message. Where you were born, what you had as a child was just plain luck: remember that. And if you give somebody else an opportunity, everybody wins in the end.

EDITOR'S NOTES

Eyal reminds us that we need to specialize before we can achieve influence. Many other contributors agree that influence is not a viable goal on its own. Like Eyal, Hurt and McGarry iterate that solid metrics and data are crucial for managing 21st-century companies.

> **"If you give somebody else an opportunity, everybody wins in the end."**
>
> **—Gil Eyal**

"I want to bottle the 'aha' leadership communication moments that can change the course of careers and deliver them to as many future leaders as I can."

Noah Zandan is the CEO and co-founder of Quantified Communications, the leading firm in applying innovative analytics, technology, and AI to help people benchmark their personal impact and become extraordinary communicators. Quantified Communications works globally with everyone from leaders of corporations, government organizations, and TED speakers, to tens of thousands of future leaders including college and graduate students, veterans, and scientists.

Noah has delivered TED and TED-Ed talks with over 11 million views, has spoken on the Intelligent Future at SXSW, and and has been published in *The Wall Street Journal, Harvard Business Review, The Economist*, NPR's "All Tech Considered," and more.

Noah formerly specialized in quantitative analysis on Wall Street and in private equity. He has an economics degree from Dartmouth College and an MBA from Northwestern University's Kellogg School of Management. Noah is also the founder and executive director of the Rockway Foundation, a non-profit supporting innovative educational projects in Latin America.

He lives in Austin, Texas with his amazing wife and three kids.

The Science of Influence

Noah Zandan

When I was in middle school, we took a field trip to a big city park. It was a bright, sunny day, and eight of us were exploring the woods when I spied the pond. As someone who loves swimming, I really wanted to jump in, but I could tell others wanted to continue to explore the woods. I vividly recall an internal debate in my head as I struggled to decide whether I wanted to follow along with my friends, or persuade them to follow me instead. Did I want to influence their choice or go along with the crowd?

I've always been intensely clear about what I like, believe in, and want to do, but navigating whether to do it myself, try to bring others along, or defer to others is hard for me. It's probably strange to think about this stuff when you're twelve, but that internal debate inspired a lot of my early thinking about influence. I've remained extremely curious about the dynamics of influence, which I define as the capacity to move others to action.

I have now been studying influence for over ten years. After partnering with some of the smartest and most self-aware leaders, researchers, and coaches in the world, analyzing hundreds of thousands of leaders with audience panels, and collecting over 1.5 billion datapoints, my North Star has remained constant: I want to bottle the "aha" leadership communication moments that can change the course of careers and deliver them to as many future leaders as I can. That's why I founded Quantified Communications.

Using Behavioral Science to Study Influence

Our mission at Quantified is to help millions of people become extraordinary communicators. We use innovative methods of measuring actual human

Quantified Communications Model

HOW TO SPEAK INFLUENTIALLY

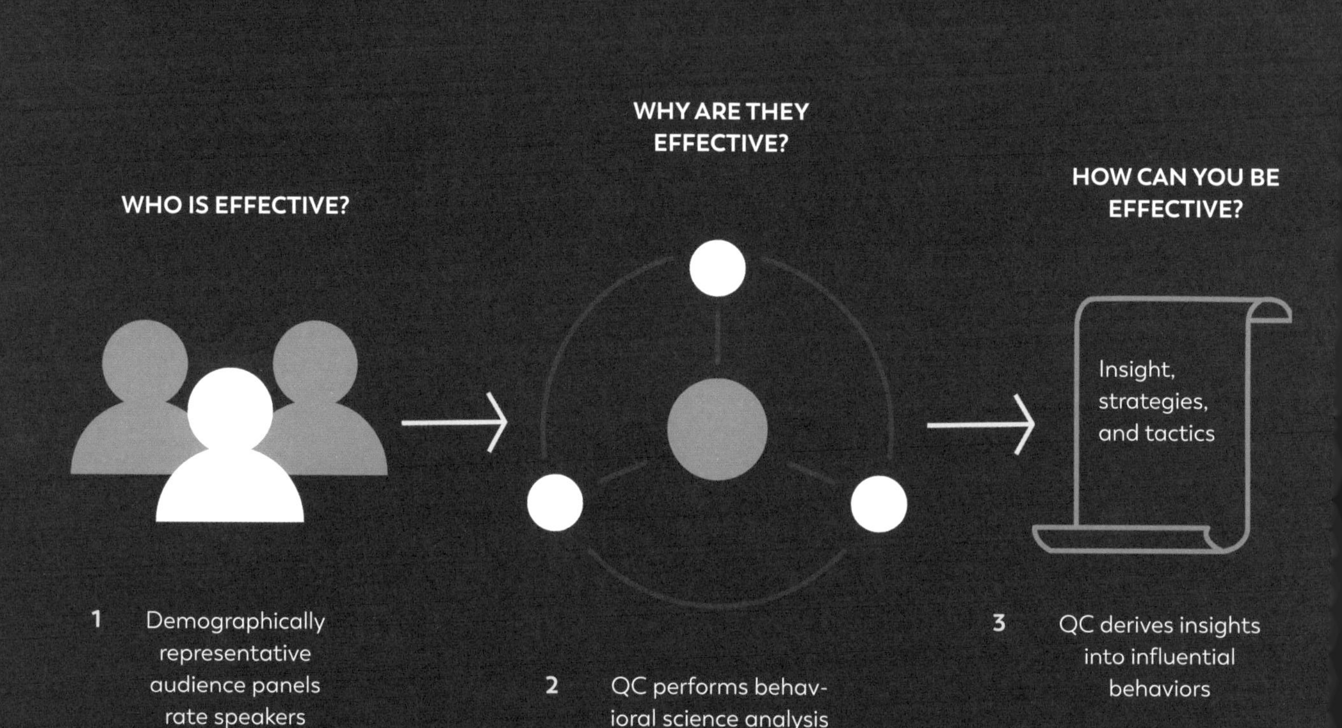

behavior and audience responses that allow us, for the first time ever, to measure, benchmark, and provide insights into how people can improve the way they communicate at incredible degrees of precision and scale. Let me explain.

Step 1: Audience Panel Review

We started by asking panels of demographically representative audiences and communication experts to rate thousands of speakers on how influential they are based on three simple questions: (1) Are you interested in hearing more from this speaker? (2) Are you influenced by this speaker? (3) Are you motivated to action by this speaker?

Once we knew which speakers the audience considered influential, our goal was to discover what specific communication behaviors—including both content and delivery—inspired interest and action. Our theory was that if we could isolate these behaviors, we could teach others how to replicate them. In other words, we could learn how to coach influence.

Step 2: Behavioral Science Measurement

Once we had our panel results, we used computational social science, also called behavioral science, to analyze the same pieces of content on more than a thousand behaviors each. What words were used? How were those words structured? Did the speaker tell stories or use facts? What did the speaker sound like, including pitch, rate, and tone of voice? Did they maintain eye contact with the audience, and did their facial expressions match the tone of the message?

Step 3: Influence Insights.

Here's what we found.

When we looked at how audiences rate speakers on influence, we found that three primary characteristics explain over 75 percent of what drives influence:

1. Engaging
2. Credible
3. Memorable

Fortunately, all three of the traits above are consistent with social science research.

But here's the thing: using the behavioral science tools and expert skill sets that make Quantified so unique in the industry, we are able to dive deeper into these three characteristics to discover the conscious and subconscious behaviors that make leaders actually come across as engaging, credible, and memorable. That's what I'd like to share here, for the first time ever. And further, our machine learning models led us to a few surprising "behavioral insights" that I'll sprinkle in along the way.

Influence Strategy #1: People (and their brains) make decisions largely by feeling rather than thinking, so start by engaging their emotions

There's a mountain of communication science research that has looked at the role emotions play in persuasion, memory, negotiation, and entertainment, and here's the big takeaway: Audiences are more likely to make decisions based on emotions as opposed to reason. The most influential people connect with their audiences on a highly emotional level.

We can clearly see this in the communication practices of renowned leaders. Using Fortune's Greatest Leaders ranking, we analyzed the speech patterns of these powerful individuals and found that they were almost three times more likely to appeal to emotion versus logic. [Figure 1]

And why is that important? Because of a phenomenon called emotional contagion. If you've ever felt like somebody's excitement—or bad mood—was contagious, then you've experienced

FIGURE 1: WORD CHOICES OF TOP SPEAKERS

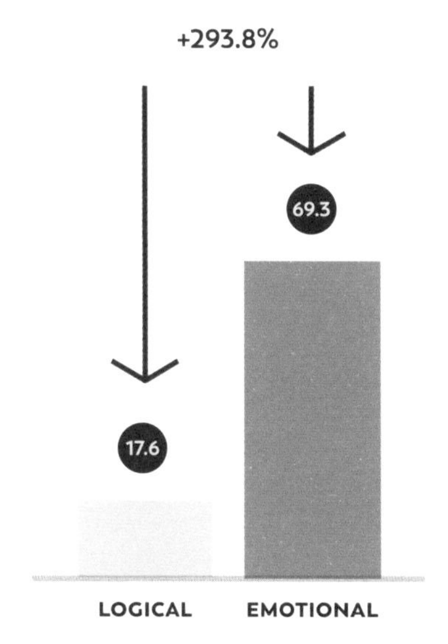

this phenomenon, which refers to the "sharing" of emotions among groups. When we engage with our audience's emotions by letting them see ours clearly, they connect with our message on a deeper level: their brain waves begin to mirror ours and, as a result, our message is more likely to change their thoughts or behavior. (You can read more about the mapping of temporal receptive windows and two-brain communication in neuroscience research from Uri Hasson at Princeton University.) Audiences feel profoundly satisfied and compelled to act when they can synchronize with a speaker whose passion for the subject is on clear display.

So how do the best communicators create emotional engagement?

Behavioral Tactic 1: Use emotional words to stir emotional responses

When we analyzed the language of the top 10 percent of influential leaders in our database as compared to everyday speakers, we found that top leaders used 3.8 percent more emotionally charged words and phrases than the average speaker, dedicating about 4 percent of their total content to words that evoke emotion. But what does that look like, exactly?

Positive Emotional Words

- Jaw-dropping
- Awe-inspiring
- Ravishing
- Gorgeous
- Delicious

“One of the biggest factors driving influence and credibility is a speaker’s ability to quote others.”

Negative Emotional Words

- Hateful
- Worthless
- Hurtful
- Ugly
- Nasty
- Gut-wrenching

The language they use is critical. Emotional language comes in several varieties. It can evoke vivid images or add drama, turning "less than ideal" into "infuriating" or "satisfied with" to "couldn't be more excited about." The best speakers use emotional language to stimulate the audience to see, hear, feel, and even smell their ideas.

Getting the language right is not always easy. John Pollack, author of *Shortcut: How Analogies Reveal Connection, Spark Innovation, and Sell Our Greatest Ideas*, points to the Ford Motor Company's failed PR campaign around the release of the 1957 Edsel. The campaign targeted "upwardly mobile" drivers by using evocative language comparing the taillights to the "graceful wingspread of a sea gull" and noting that the front grille provided a "distinctive continental flair." Ford didn't release any images of the car ahead of time, and its vivid campaign language influenced hordes of customers to rush to the showrooms once the vehicle was unveiled.

Unfortunately, the public didn't buy into Ford's descriptions, and instead invented analogies of their own. They compared the car's features to a "dirty horse collar" and "a soiled toilet seat." While Ford's evocative imagery set one tone for the vehicle, the raw emotion in the public's language won out, and the Edsel was ultimately a failure.

The Edsel's failure makes sense in light of data we now have. Quantified's machine learning models have shown a surprising connection between influence and negative language, which inspires emotion and engagement: the most influential leaders use 34 percent more negative language than everyday speakers.

Behavioral Tactic 2: Vocal variety is the key to subconsciously engaging your audience

But emotional language isn't the only factor in persuasive speaking. Influential communicators also allow language to play out in the way they speak—their vocal tone, facial expressions, and gestures. If a speaker is slumped at a podium and speaking in a monotone, audiences are going to have a hard time believing he's invested in what he has to say. But if the speaker is standing upright, maybe even leaning forward just a bit, and allowing her emotions to play into her facial expressions and gestures and the way she uses her voice, then audiences are likely to respond.

Of course, these emotional appeals can be supported by images, music, and videos as needed (for inspiration, just think of the last ASPCA commercial you saw), but emotional contagion starts with your verbal and nonverbal cues, and the key is variety. Our brains love surprises.

SPEAKERS WE ADMIRE

Malala Yousafzai's passion has always been one of her defining leadership characteristics. In her 2013 speech at the Youth Takeover of the United Nations, she used a whopping 67.1 percent more emotionally charged language than the average speaker.

Caroline Rothstein, a New York City writer and performer, is credited with inspiring young women to feel confident about their own bodies, thanks largely to the viral YouTube video in which she talks about her own battle with bulimia. In this video she uses 30.5 percent more emotionally charged language than the average leader, helping her rack up millions of views.

“63 percent remember the stories, while only 5 percent recall any individual data point.”

Diving into the data, we found that the top 10 percent of influential leaders in our database use 70 percent more vocal variety, including tone and emotion, than the average speaker.

So next time you're sharing an important position, don't hesitate to express your passion and make your feelings known by replacing some of your even-keeled, professional language and tone with words, images, nonverbal signals, and vocal qualities that help your audience connect with how you're really feeling.

Influence Strategy #2: Back Up Your Engaging Communication with Credibility

The first question any communicator has to answer—especially for an unfamiliar audience—is, "Why should anyone listen to what I have to say?"

In order to be influential, a leader has to be credible. Credibility is the audience's perception that a speaker is a reliable authority on the subject at hand. Their content references experience, credible sources, and detail. Their delivery is confident, open, and authentic.

This is key because audiences don't want to analyze—they want to intuit. Daniel Kahneman has done some amazing research into deep versus intuitive thinking and our brains' preference for the latter. What it comes down to is that in order to trust a speaker and allow themselves to be influenced by her, audiences need to intuitively believe that what she's saying is accurate. And the easiest way to convince an audience of that is to build credibility.

Now, if you're a rock star in your field, if you're speaking inside the red circle at TED, or if you've been working with your particular audience for years, you may have already built all the credibility you need. But if you and your audience are new to each other, if you're introducing a new idea or project or role to a familiar audience, or if you're at an earlier stage in your career, then building a little credibility will go a long way in getting listeners on board. So, now the question is, how do you build credibility?

Behavioral Tactic 1: Show your audience the value you can provide for them

In order to get anyone on board with your vision, you'll need to show them why they should be involved and why they should care. Imagine a sales rep going on and on about his company's innovative technology and all its bells and whistles, when the real question on the potential customer's mind is, "How can this help me?"

When Quantified looked at the behavioral science underlying credibility, we discovered a fascinating tactic: you can build credibility with an audience by talking about them and their daily experience. We found that the top 10 percent of influential leaders use 62 percent more personalized language and

SPEAKERS WE ADMIRE

Brené Brown is one of our favorite communicators. She's a speaker, researcher, and author who's a pro at establishing credibility. She outlines her bona fides upfront, without just reciting her resume or bragging about her accomplishments. Despite having a PhD, she uses simple language to do it. For an example, check out her 2010 TEDxHouston talk.

Bryan Stevenson, a human rights attorney, is a master of storytelling. In his eighteen-minute TED Talk on America's justice system, he used three compelling personal stories. Audience members were so inspired that they donated $1 million to Stevenson's nonprofit, the Equal Justice Initiative. That's influence in action.

35 percent more second-person pronouns (such as you and your) than the average speaker.

When you focus on an audience instead of yourself, you become someone credible—someone they want to listen to and support. What is their life like? What is their day like? What are their frustrations? What do they care about?

I once saw author and speaker Simon Sinek do this masterfully in a roomful of CEOs. He said simply, "I'm happy to talk about my books, my work, my research, but I know what you deal with on a daily basis, and I do what I do to be of service to you as leaders. So what concerns do you have, and how can I help?" The CEO next to me actually leaned over and said, "Who is this guy?" which I think is exactly the response Sinek was hoping for.

Behavioral Tactic 2: Lean on the credibility of others

Often, building credibility comes down to proving we know our stuff. If your audience doesn't yet know you as an expert, you can show them by leaning on external research and the work of top practitioners to show that you've done your homework. You can also reference awards, accolades, and testimonials you've received to show that other known experts have vouched for you.

It's actually fairly simple: to be credible in the eyes of an audience, use evidence they already find credible.

Though leaning on third-party credibility is a fairly intuitive tactic, our machine learning analysis revealed that one of the biggest factors driving influence and credibility is a speaker's ability to quote others. The most influential leaders in our study used 85 percent more quotations than the average speaker.

When an audience doesn't recognize you quite yet as a credible expert, associating yourself with words and ideas they've already accepted from people they've already embraced works as a shortcut to convincing your audience that you're also worth listening to.

Behavioral Tactic 3: To be credible, be clear

Credibility doesn't come from complexity. As Mark Twain said, "Don't use a five-dollar word when a fifty-cent word will do." Being clear with your audience, both in your beliefs and your message, is critical for building credibility. If your content is convoluted—if it's unclear what your purpose is or if the audience has trouble following along with what you're saying—they'll write you off as not worth the effort.

We see influential leaders use 17 percent clearer language than the average speaker.

So if you want to be clear (and thus credible), do three things when you speak:

1. Keep the structure simple. Use fewer words per sentence and fewer syllables per word

2. Be sure your content is organized logically and coherently. Guide your audience from A to Z. If you bring up an idea, follow it with an outcome, and be sure causes have effects.
3. Distill abstract ideas into simple, concrete terms. Use simple action verbs that appeal to the senses.

The clearer you are, the more in control and knowledgeable you will come across, and the more confident and willing the audience will be to engage with what you have to say.

If you focus on building your credibility as a speaker or leader, your audience will start to see you as someone they should listen to and someone with ideas worth considering. In other words, as someone influential.

Influence Strategy #3: At the end of the day, none of it matters if it's not memorable

People act on what they remember, not on what they forget. The Darwinian reason we need memory of the past is so we can inform the future.

But getting into people's heads is not so simple. One of my favorite researchers is Leonard Mlodinow, and in his book *Subliminal* he shares that about 95 percent of the energy your brain uses goes toward unconscious processes. And the conscious processes only take up about 5 percent of your brain. So if the unconscious is really what runs the human body, then to be memorable, we have to impact the subconscious. Here's how:

Behavioral Tactic 1: Repeat, repeat, repeat

Memorable leaders deliver the same message to every audience, every time. They stick to their values and demonstrate authenticity and self-discipline.

Of course, this doesn't mean they're giving stump speeches—every communication event is personalized to a particular audience's needs and values. But the core of the message remains the same, no matter who the leader is talking to or how unpopular that message might be.

When we look at the data, we found the most influential leaders use 54 percent fewer jargon words and 34 percent fewer vague generalities than the average speaker—they get to the point rather than dancing around it. And then they reinforce it.

Take JPMorgan Chase CEO Jamie Dimon, for example. Dimon is known as a remarkable communicator, largely due to his message consistency, especially with the unhesitating way he expresses unpopular or controversial opinions. From disagreements with the president's financial, ideological, and leadership policies to his harsh criticism of bitcoin (which J.P. Morgan still trades), Dimon's communication is simple, informal, and consistent.

Behavioral Tactic 2: Memory starts with eye contact

While we know eye contact is an important speaking behavior, we were surprised to find how closely it's related to memorability. When we look at the machine learning insights on memorability, we see that speakers who make great eye contact are considered memorable. The top 10 percent of influential leaders make 47 percent better eye contact than the average speaker.

Maintaining strong eye contact is one of the most visible ways to showcase your confidence and connect with your audience, but I would not have guessed that it influenced memorability as well.

Behavioral Tactic 3: A straight path to recall is storytelling, and the secret to storytelling is called a story file

In his book *Made to Stick*, Chip Heath, a professor of organizational behavior at Stanford, talks about an experiment that demonstrates how we remember speeches. He asks his students to make one-minute presentations in support or opposition of the idea that violent crime is a serious problem in the United States. Later in the day, after the class has moved on to other topics, he asks students to write down everything they can remember about the presentations their classmates gave. The students, he says, are shocked at how little they can remember. But here's the kicker: the students tend to use 2.5 statistics in their one-minute speeches, and only one in ten tells an emotional story. Conversely, when he asks students to recall what they've heard, 63 percent remember the stories, while only 5 percent recall any individual data point.

Whether you are listening to someone speak or reading a book, when you are immersed in that story, there are two things happening in your brain.

On a neurological level, your brain activity increases dramatically. When you hear straight facts, you use the language processing and language comprehension centers of your brain. But when you listen to stories, you also engage your motor cortex and your emotion and visual image processing centers to imagine sensations and process emotional reactions. As you focus on the story, your brain is working harder, and as a result, you are more likely to recall the messages later.

Meanwhile, at the chemical level, your brain is releasing oxytocin, the bonding hormone that causes you to care about the people involved. This reaction is why you sometimes treat your favorite fictional characters as real people, why sharing personal stories is the fastest way to bond with strangers, and why storytelling is a politician's best weapon. Not only are you hearing about somebody's experience, but you're living it right along with them. The more of their experience you share, the more oxytocin is released, and the more likely you are to internalize that story, think about it later, and act on it.

Storytelling is the not-so-secret ingredient that makes the difference between being a manager and being a leader, between delivering remarks and being an extraordinary speaker. Research shows stories are twenty-two times more memorable than just facts.

What, exactly, makes a good story? There are numerous books available on the subject, but in short, make sure your story has a clear beginning, middle, and end. Start by establishing the setting and introducing tension through conflict. Move toward the turning point, when the tension is at its highest, and nail the climax. Follow up with a resolution that establishes a new normal for the characters.

Now, your upcoming corporate presentation won't be the next Great American Novel, but use this structure, and wrap your key points into short "storylets" by sharing specific details that humanize your message. You might share the inspiration behind a new corporate policy, talk about the team members who stepped up and made a difference in a recent initiative, and colorfully describe the efforts that led to your success (or failure).

When you package your message as a story, your audience will be able to put themselves in your shoes, connecting with your message on a personal, emotional level that will make them more likely to remember what you had to say and buy in to your ideas.

But here's the thing: Very few people can create great stories in their heads in real time. Stories are almost always pre-prepared by great speakers. Speaker coaches call this your "story-file." Creating two or three stories, writing them down, and accessing them at appropriate moments will put you immediately ahead of the pack.

Your actions inspire others

My favorite definition of leadership is from the sixth president of the United States, John Quincy Adams: "If your actions inspire others to dream more, learn more, do more, and become more, you are a leader."

You don't have to sit in the C-suite to be a leader, and you don't have to be the smartest person in the room. Our research shows that leaders are those who can clearly communicate their ideas, hopes, concerns, and plans in a way that captures the hearts and minds of would-be followers. Ultimately, the successful leader moves people to action.

If I could go back to middle school, I would tell myself to get out of my head and follow my natural inclinations. My friends all knew that I loved to swim. Instead of debating with myself whether it was a moment to lead or follow, I could have simply expressed my passion for swimming. Rather than worrying and analyzing and thinking about leadership, I should have been leading authentically, by feeling and expressing.

I hope these insights—the result of my personal curiosity and research on what makes the best leaders so effective and influential—are helpful as you accelerate your path to achieving your potential and improving our world.

What Sets the Most Influential Speakers Apart?

Compared to the average speaker, the top 10 percent of influential leaders use:

3x more emotional words than logical ones

85% more quotations

62% more personalized language

54% fewer jargon words

47% better eye contact

35% more "you" and "your" pronouns

34% fewer vague generalities

17% clearer language

Closing Thoughts

Insights into Influence started with the idea of collecting stories and insights from leading thinkers and practitioners on the subject of influencing other people's behavior.

The definition of influence is remarkably consistent across our contributors, as is the caution that influence can be exerted both positively and negatively. Influence is a skill we all possess from birth, although it is a devilishly sophisticated skill to develop and hone. The best influencers are able to transform the thinking and behavior of large groups of people, not by forcing them but by inspiring them. As with any complex skill, the ability to influence others requires insight, technique, direction, and intentional development. Influence is a practice—like leadership or yoga—that can be strengthened and deepened with time and experience.

At Weeva, we strive to collect rich content that people find useful for achieving significant impact in the world. We care intensely about creating deeper connection and meaning between people and adding back something both thoughtful and beautiful to the world. Accordingly, *Insights into Influence* collects the thinking of the top neuroscientists, social scientists, and practitioners working in the field today.

We are deeply indebted to every contributor for the wonderful content within this book. Thank you to our experts for generously sharing your current research, insights, and personal experiences on how to develop influence skills. This book would not be possible without you.

Thank you to our amazing partner, Noah Zandan at Quantified Communications, for believing in this book and bringing it to fruition. The incredible network of experts you've built, and the deep analysis and insight you've brought to the field already, have had an outsized impact on people wishing to develop and practice the skills of influence. From our very first meeting, you shared your passion and commitment to developing the skills of effective leadership, and it has been our pleasure to work with you.

Sarah, thank you for working so enthusiastically and creatively on all elements of this project. It has been a treat to get to know you and to sample your awesome range of talents. Thank you for your tireless efforts on editing and proofing the book, and for the constant flow of ideas on how to make the book better.

I want to give a big shout out to the Weeva team as well. Margaret, we came to rely on your editing superpowers in record time. Thanks also for taking on the heavy lifting of weaving the stories together and sequencing and recapping them so well.

Cassidy, you are a wonderfully talented designer. It is fantastic to see you grow as an artist and as an accomplished professional. Rachel, you've been a fantastic addition to team Weeva, contributing right away to this project as well as others. I'm delighted to have you both on our team.

Tuscan, you are our rock and our all-around all-star. You are technical, creative, pragmatic, and versatile. That's a wonderful combination. We count on you every day and are so grateful you are a member of Weeva's founding team.

Last but not least, thank you to our readers. In your own quest to become extraordinary influencers, may you find the content in this volume insightful, practical, and actionable. We welcome your feedback on this book and also your wish list for future volumes.

Now, let's put these ideas into practice and change the world for good.

Sincerely,

KIM GORSUCH
Founder and CEO of Weeva, Inc.

Kimberly Gorsuch

P.S. If you or someone you know wants to make their very own book, we'd be delighted to explore it. Reach out to us at Hello@Weeva.com.

About the Author

Noah Zandan is the CEO and co-founder of Quantified Communications, the leading firm in applying innovative analytics, technology, and AI to help people benchmark their personal impact and become extraordinary communicators. Quantified Communications works globally with everyone from leaders of corporations, government organizations, and TED speakers, to tens of thousands of future leaders including college and graduate students, veterans, and scientists.

Noah has delivered TED and TED-Ed talks with over 11 million views, has spoken on the Intelligent Future at SXSW, and and has been published in The Wall Street Journal, Harvard Business Review, The Economist, NPR's "All Tech Considered," and more.

Noah formerly specialized in quantitative analysis on Wall Street and in private equity. He has an economics degree from Dartmouth College and an MBA from Northwestern University's Kellogg School of Management. Noah is also the founder and executive director of the Rockway Foundation, a non-profit supporting innovative educational projects in Latin America.

He lives in Austin, Texas with his amazing wife and three kids.

Credits

Noah Zandan
Author and Executive Producer

Kim Gorsuch
Publisher and Executive Producer

Sarah Welch
Executive Editor

Margaret Collins
Editor

Cassidy Reynolds
Lead Designer

Tuscan Knox
Cover Designer

Rachel Bostick
Designer

Ethan Burris, PhD, and Deb Ploskonka
Data Analysis

Quantified Communications Team, Past and Present
Research and Development

Notes

Notes

COLLECTING AND COMPOSING THE WORLD'S MOST POWERFUL STORIES

We hope you have enjoyed reading this anthology of Insights into Influence as much as we have enjoyed creating it.

We believe that working together as communities, colleagues, and friends to make awesome books is a truly special way of collaborating as humans.

Our goal at Weeva is to deepen connection and meaning between people through authentic and collaborative storytelling. We make it easy and fast for you to create your very own book. Use our online turnkey platform to collect the wisdom, experience, and stories that you want to preserve, then let our professional editors and designers transform your content into beautiful, shareable artifacts. We'll incorporate your brand standards and reflect back the personality of your organization.

We believe books are the perfect complement to the temporal stream of digital consciousness. Books encourage people to pause in time, and our lusciously printed editions encourage prime placement on a coffee table or desk, keeping your company and its messaging powerfully present.

If you have a book project in mind, we'd be delighted to explore it with you. Reach out to us at **Hello@Weeva.com**.

We hope to connect with you soon!

www.weeva.com